FINDING ME

Finding ME

How I Ended the War Inside My Mind to
Show You How to End Yours

RYAN LIGHTHOUSE

Lighthouse Leadership Publishing

Lighthouse Leadership Publishing

Printed in the United States of America

Paperback ISBN 979-8-9996422-0-2
Ebook ISBN 979-8-9996422-1-9

Dedicated to my Pachú

The journey to find ME started so I could be here to meet YOU.

Contents

I'm Still Here

It was 8:18 PM on April 7th, 2025. I was folding laundry.

Two years after my breakdown, one year after my son was born, six months after I'd finally sold my business and committed fully to this new path . . .

Ordinary task. Nothing poetic. Just the background noise of a Tuesday. A forgotten corner of life where the mundane meets the unconscious. But sometimes, that's exactly where the deepest truths hide.

Somewhere in the rhythm of shirts and socks, in the simple motion of fold and place, fold and place, something started to stir inside me. Thoughts moved in like fog rolling across a still lake. Quiet but thick.

I started reflecting.

About the work I'd been doing. The researching. The studying. The hours spent writing. The endless journaling. The late-night realizations I didn't always understand but wrote down anyway. The quiet mornings where I pulled thoughts from places I didn't know existed. Places that didn't feel like they were mine, but somehow . . . were.

What's it all for?

That question landed like a thunderclap in a cathedral.

And then, it came.

"I'm here, I'm here, I'm here."

A whisper—soft at first. Familiar. Ancient. It didn't scare me. It didn't startle me. It filled me.

Then it grew louder:

"I'm here! I'm here! I'm here!"

And then it screamed—not in anger, but in joy:

"I'm still fucking here! Isn't this beautiful!?"

At first, I thought it was my Wounded Child finally speaking up. The part of me that had gone silent decades ago, buried under layers of performance, pressure, and pain.

But it wasn't him.

It was ME.

My voice. My real voice. The one I hadn't heard in over three decades. Not the voice I used to pitch, sell, convince, or coach. Not the voice I'd trained to be on camera or show up to lead masterminds.

This was the voice I came into the world with. Pure. Whole. Untouched.

And in that moment, I whispered back:

"I know man, I'm still here too."

That's why this book exists.

Not for marketing. Not for positioning. Not for some slick new funnel. Not to get more clients. Not to add "author" to my Instagram bio— **it's for that moment right there.**

This book exists because I finally heard the one voice that matters: the one I lost, the one I silenced, the one I've been unknowingly searching for since I was a child.

For the first time in over thirty years, I heard my True Self.

Loud. Clear. Free.

And he had something to say.

This book is that message.

You'll meet the voices that shaped me. The parts I played. The chaos I wrote my way through. And the map I built from the ruins.

This is the story of *how I wrote my way back to ME.*

A recovery manual disguised as a memoir. A time capsule of mental healing for the man who feels like his mind has turned against him. For the one who built the metaphorical empire but lost themselves in the process. Climbed the mountain but forgot why they were climbing it to begin with. For the ones who achieved everything they set out to do . . . and still felt empty.

If you've ever felt like you're performing success while quietly falling apart . . . If you've ever built everything and still felt like nothing . . . If you've ever stared at the ceiling at 3 AM wondering if there's someone else upstairs . . . fearful something is wrong with you . . . If you've ever heard a whisper in the dark and thought, *"Is the real me still in there?"*

Then this isn't just my story. It's yours too.

By understanding the journey I took to find ME, I am hoping that you will be able to continue the journey to finding YOU.

The War Nobody Sees

From the outside, my childhood looked normal.

Middle-class family. Decent grades. Played sports. No abuse. No addiction. No tragic story that would make the evening news. By all societal standards, a *normal* kid growing up in suburban America with parents who stayed together, food on the table, and a roof over his head.

So why did I feel like I was dying inside?

This is the story most men never tell—not because it's too dramatic, but because it seems too ordinary. We look at our *"normal"* childhoods and think we have no right to feel broken. We compare our experience to the endless tragedy streamed across the television twenty-four hours a day. In a world filled with so many *big* problems there's no room for the *small* ones of our minds. At least that's what our modern society would lead us to believe. In the end, leaving a generation of children to grow to become lost adults. No understanding of the war raging in our minds. No explanation for why success feels empty and achievement feels like armor.

The mind doesn't need extreme trauma to fracture. It just needs a sensitive soul and a few careless words at the wrong time.

A parent's harsh criticism at a critical moment. The pressure to be less sensitive, less curious, less yourself. The slow, systematic teaching that who you are isn't quite right. That if you want to fit in, you need to be different, better, more like someone else.

These aren't the kind of wounds that show up on x-rays. They're the kind that split you into pieces from the inside.

The Cast You'll Meet

That splitting created the cast of characters you'll meet in this book. Not imaginary friends or creative metaphors. But, the very real parts of me that emerged to handle what the whole of me couldn't.

The Wounded Child who got locked away—the sensitive boy who asked too many questions and felt too deeply. But locking someone away doesn't make them disappear. He speaks through fear and sadness, through poetry and pain, through midnight anxiety and 3 AM tears.

The Protector emerged to protect him—the part that decided if being myself meant rejection, then I'd become someone no one could reject. Angry. Driven. Invulnerable. He speaks through achievement and aggression, through the need to dominate before being dominated.

The Brain became my escape route—if I couldn't feel safe being myself, maybe I could think my way to safety. Strategic. Analytical. Always ten steps ahead but never present. He speaks through endless calculations and mental models, building elaborate strategies to avoid feeling.

And then there's **ME**—not another part, but what was left of my authentic self. The voice that got buried under all the armor and adaptation. The one who finally whispered "I'm still here" after three decades of silence.

These parts aren't unique to me. You have them too. Different names, maybe. Different origin stories. But the same basic architecture of a mind that learned to divide itself to survive experiences that looked normal from the outside but felt like death from within.

This isn't just a book about trauma. It's a book about the stories our minds create from our unique experiences. Stories powerful enough to split us into pieces. Stories that run our lives from the shadows until we finally find the courage to read them clearly.

Most men are fighting a war nobody else can see. Performing success while falling apart inside. Building empires while losing themselves. Looking completely normal while feeling completely fractured. Hanging on by a thread as they lose control of the facade they've held together for protection.

If that's you, then this isn't just my story.

It's ours.

And it's time to understand the battlefield.

A Word Before We Begin

When you read these pages, you'll likely feel a lot of things. Recognition. Confusion. Relief. Maybe even anger or sadness. It's normal. Those emotions aren't obstacles to understanding, they're signposts. They're your parts talking. Listen to them. The more you read, the more you will understand.

Here's how to get the most out of this experience:

1.   **Read with your whole body, not just your mind.** When something hits you, don't just intellectualize it. Feel where it lands in your body. That tightness in your chest? That heat in your face? That's where your work is.

2.   **Stop when you need to.** When you hit a section that makes your mind race or your heart pound, put the book down. Step away. Process. Come back when you're ready. This isn't a race.

3.   **Answer the reflection questions.** I've included questions at the end of each chapter that force you to look in the mirror. Don't skip them. Don't just think about them. Write your answers down. The act of writing bypasses your Brain's automatic bullshit detector and taps into something more authentic.

4.   **Use the tools.** The downloadable diagrams, worksheets and exercises aren't bonus material — they're essential components. This book isn't about understanding my journey; it's about starting yours.

https://www.ryanlighthouse.com/findingme

5.   **Trust resistance.** When a part of you screams "This is stupid" or "This doesn't apply to me," pay attention. That's usually when you're closest to something important. Your Protector is on high alert because something vulnerable is close to the surface.

The goal isn't perfection. It's recognition.

Seeing yourself clearly, possibly for the first time.

You don't need to solve everything in these pages. You just need to start noticing the patterns. The walls. The armor. The performances. All the ways you've learned to be perfect at being someone other than yourself.

I'm not your guru. I'm not your therapist. I'm just a guy who found his way back to himself after decades of being lost. And I'm here to tell you: the path isn't pretty, but it's worth every uncomfortable step.

This is the future that's possible when you release your mind from the baggage weighing it down and open it up to unlock the genius capability inside.

This truly is the master key to the greatest gift this life and every life after has to offer.

If you have the desire to Listen and Learn, the Will to Understand by traversing the one inch between you and everything you can imagine you can become, I promise you that you can find your own master key.

And, with it, unlock the door to the genius who resides within.

Let's begin. It's time.

Part One

Losing ME

CHAPTER 1

The First Split . . . of Many

Before the world hardened me, there was a boy who was just . . . himself. Curious. Creative. Free. ME. This is the story of how that boy died. How I killed him. Or at least, how I thought I did. How I found him again.

More importantly . . . ***how I brought him back.***

I heard my name called and made my way to the front of the room to receive my end-of-year trophy. Each of my football coaches stood there to greet me. Standing tall with smiles on their faces as they shared their own little spiel about coaching me.

They spoke about my curiosity as a player. The questions I would ask about each play. The "ideas" I would share with them that I came up with on my own. They laughed—caringly—as they described this "different" type of player they had on their team.

When I reached the stage, I shook hands with each coach, thanked them for a great season, and nervously made my way back to my seat. I was just a little "shy," as my mom would say. I returned to my seat next to my parents.

I don't remember what they said when I sat down. But I remember what came next.

I stood next to my father as we watched a good friend of mine receive his trophy. As he walked to the front of the room, the coaches described his tenacity on the field. How he followed every directive precisely. They said he would run through a brick wall if they told him to.

That's when I heard six words that I'll never forget. From a voice that I couldn't believe was saying them.

"Why can't you be more like that?"

Those six words taught me a devastating lesson: being myself wasn't enough. I had to be perfect—perfect according to others' standards, not my own. I intuitively understood that anything less than perfection meant rejection. And rejection, to my young mind, felt like death.

I don't remember anything from the evening after that. What I do remember is that was the first time I killed myself. And it wouldn't be the last.

The part of me that died that day wouldn't return until I discovered him locked away inside the prison of my mind decades later. Screaming for help. Begging to be set free. Begging to know—*why did you put me here?*

This split inside me manifested in ways I wouldn't understand until years later. I began making conscious choices to hide parts of myself—not just my sensitivity, but my intelligence too.

I remember back in sixth grade, I was supposed to take some accelerated test. The kind that would put me in classes with the "smart kids." I purposely failed it. Not because I couldn't pass—because I didn't want to. All of my friends at that time were in a program called "resource." A special program in school to provide extra help and tutoring for kids who were struggling.

Being labeled as "too smart" would have been just as dangerous as being "too sensitive." It would have separated me from my friends. Leaving me alone. Exposed. Back in the firing line for more pain.

So I dimmed myself. Deliberately. I learned which parts of me were acceptable to show and which needed to stay hidden.

This pattern would follow me throughout my life—this intuitive understanding that parts of me needed to be suppressed, hidden away, locked in that mental prison cell. My curiosity, my sensitivity, my intelligence—these were vulnerabilities in a world that valued toughness, simplicity, fitting in.

Before the Armor

Let me take you back to what life was like before all of the splits.

I was always different. Even as a little kid, I felt everything more intensely than others seemed to. I would walk into a room and feel the energy shift. I could sense when something bad was about to happen before it did. I just felt these things.

I can remember a traumatizing experience going to a haunted house at my mother's work as a child. She worked at Upstate Cerebral Palsy and the haunted house was operated by the patients who stayed on campus. The way I would describe the experience is this: *"It was like I could hear the screams of desperate souls trapped inside a paralyzed mind."* I feel the same thing today with my grandfather who has Alzheimer's.

My mind worked differently, too. I asked "why" about everything. I wanted to understand how things worked, why people did what they did. I wasn't satisfied with "because I said so" or "that's just how it is." I needed to know more.

Unfortunately, the environment that I grew up in didn't value that type of thinking. You were expected to do what you were told. Questioning was seen as defiance. Even if that questioning came from a place of innocence.

Throughout my story you will encounter a series of significant emotional events that I've identified as key points in shaping my identity. While these events were significant and impactful themselves, the environment that you exist in will provide the most consistent pressures to ultimately shape who you are.

It also provides the answers to why you are, who you are . . .

In my recent studies of Psychosomatic Medicine and the work of doctor John Sarno, I found it fascinating that some of the doctors he trained said the most profound change they made to the way they treated their patients was taking a social history and description of personality. They said it was this information that gave them the most clues to whether or not someone should be diagnosed with TMS (Tension myositis syndrome, a type of psychogenic chronic pain).

Which is why I feel it's important to share about my family history. They did play a vital role in shaping me into the person I am today, of course. Plus, there may be a pattern that emerges for you to see and connect with in your own family history.

Disclaimer: The following section is sharing my personal perspective on the people in the environment I grew up in. It is in no way meant to harm, attack, or create conflict with anyone mentioned. This is simply my perspective on my own individual human experience. I am aware of and open to any other perspectives that may exist outside of my own. So, I say all that to say, this doesn't mean I'm right. It's just how my mind experienced the world from the inside out.

The Environment That Molded ME

As I look back on my childhood I can remember a very happy period which came to a stop sometime around the age of six to ten years old.

Unfortunately, the intensity of the negative often overshadows the frequency of the positive. So, many of my positive memories are nothing more than a blur. Before doing the work and reintegrating myself, they were non-existent.

Growing up in my household was exactly what you expect in a 'law enforcement' family home. My father worked for the US Marshals Service which meant we were a home of rigid rules and conservative values. Church on Sunday was a requirement. Or Saturday evening, if you didn't want to wake up in the morning.

Looking back, I guess you would say there was an image to uphold. Clean cut, well behaved, Catholic values and respect for the rule of law. At home my dad was the ruler and he had some very strict laws. Some we knew about and some we didn't. I call those unspoken contracts (there will be more on those in *Finding YOU*). To explain the overall vibe of the household I think the following story should suffice.

A popular story told in my household was about the discipline and structure with which my great-grandfather ran his household. It goes like this:

Each night when my great-grandfather arrived home from work it was expected that his dinner was on the table and all the children were silently in their rooms. So he could eat in peace and quiet after working all day. If this wasn't the case, there would be consequences.

While my house was never run exactly like that, if you heard the pride in my father's voice as he told that story you would understand. It was told as if it was something to aspire to. Also, my great-grandfather was my father's best friend. Our household and the way it was run was modeled after him.

This meant that things like playing too loudly, running in the house, talking too loudly, rough housing, not listening, crying, and countless other infractions were met with an unusually high level of anger and aggression. Children are meant to be seen, not heard, as my great-grandfather would say.

While there was rarely, if ever, physical violence, the psychological fear and emotional confusion that was instilled was intense. Imagine someone angrily scolding a dog. That's how we were disciplined. You weren't disciplined by your name, you were called "boy" to dehumanize you. Or you were sent off to mom to deal with what "her son" did. When you dehumanize the target it makes escalating the violence that much easier. It also makes the guilt and shame afterward that much more tolerable.

My mom was the cushion between us to dissipate the damage from him. Except when she couldn't control us. Then, she would weaponize him against us.

"Wait till your father gets home" was the threat that stopped everything in our household. This also created the feeling *that you never wanted Dad to come home.* A weird feeling for a child to have, I think?

Do as you're told and if you don't there will be extreme consequences. That's very much the culture of men that I grew up around in my youth. You might never even find out what you did wrong sometimes, either. And what you did might be totally out of your control . . .

My older brother had really bad allergies as a kid and would be coughing up mucus most nights during spring and early summer. I have memories of my father screaming down the hallway at my brother to stop coughing so loud at night. Sometimes threatening him with punishment. Think of the confusion for a child getting screamed at for being sick.

Before you judge . . . I understand it now . . . Children are meant to be seen, not heard. Remember?

The People That Shaped ME

DAD

If I'm honest, up until the age of around six to ten my dad was my greatest hero. From then until thirty years old, my dad was the person I was most afraid of. Second to that was the darkness inside of me. Quite the irony, looking back on it.

As I became a teenager the 'fun' activities that most kids did with their dad, I did with my Uncle Bill. Baseball games, football games, movies, hiking, whitewater rafting etc. These type of activities shifted from my dad to him. He had a son that was similar in age so I guess it made sense? Looking back on it I believe it unfortunately placed my father in a single role—the disciplinarian.

Like I said, he governed with an intensity and aggressiveness that would instill fear simply from his eyes and speed of movement. He could get a dog to cower away by looking at it alone. It's in the eyes. They're piercing. Like daggers shooting into your soul showing you a glimpse of the fiery rage they carry within. A gift and a curse I now am imbued with myself.

I came to learn, as will you, that this is the embodiment of the Protector. The monster inside who is created to protect the Wounded Child—the part of you who he must make safe from whoever hurt him. My dad's story is his to tell. But, one thing I've found to hold true in all of my research is that hurt people hurt people.

While my grandparents never showed anything but love towards my brother, and I, we always heard stories. As we became adults, those stories became more of a reality. This painted a clear picture for me as to why my dad was the way he was. It also helped me overcome my own negative behaviors that I had inherited.

The monster inside of him that I was afraid of I've come to find out is a generational pattern. It recurs in our lineage. A self-perpetuating pattern of abusive behavior creating the same self-destructive patterns, of self-protection, in each generation to come.

Interestingly enough, in a conversation with my dad he shared with me that he thought by not raising his hand to us, he would end the pattern. Unfortunately, he wasn't aware that this form of psychological and emotional abuse was far more destructive than the physical parts he removed.

This is a great example of the importance of the process you're going to witness and be able to utilize for yourself with *Finding YOU*. When you understand your past it will allow you to accept your present and open the door to a new future. This deep understanding of my family history and the patterns that existed allowed me to shift from anger towards my father to empathy for him.

This understanding allowed me to appreciate his pain and why he was the way he was. Which further helped me understand who I am.

MOM

As I sit here to write this section I'm overcome with overwhelming emotion. It's interesting. Because, I have two different versions of my mom that I experienced. There was the one that I witnessed from the outside and the other that I was forced to meet from the inside.

To be honest, I wish I never met the second one.

The first version of Mom existed until my college years. She was the laid-back, outgoing, light-hearted, free-spirited, self-confident mom. The woman who would dance at a party when no one else was dancing. She was always looking to have fun and didn't care who was watching (. . . or at least so I thought).

She had the patience to do the things that Dad couldn't. Like teach me how to ride a bike, tie my shoes and cope with the world.

The second version started in college after she opened a door into her mind that I never wanted to be let into. Let's just say that after an experience you will learn about later I was able to see the underlying anxiety, self-consciousness, judgment and desperate need for love that created the behaviors above. I saw the lonely little girl, cowered away in a corner, waiting for someone to love her enough to set her free.

Knowing the environment she grew up in, it makes perfect sense. Again, my mom's story is her own, but it's important to understand her history for mine. My mom's mom, my grandmother, came from an abusive household and had to go live with her relatives as a young child.

As you can imagine, for my grandmother the entire idea of love was foreign. In thirty-seven years, I've never heard my grandmother say "I love you" or voluntarily kiss or hug anyone. Knowing what I know now, I feel extreme empathy and sadness for her.

My grandfather didn't necessarily make up for what she lacked with his emotions. His family was very wealthy and lived a high-class lifestyle until the Great Depression. Almost overnight, they lost everything. His mother never forgave his father for losing their wealth and status. I believe he and his brother received their own version of her anger and my grandfather was forever fearful of losing it all.

Although they were emotionally distant, my brother and I always saw their soft souls buried under the callused shell their life experience created. I never saw them behave in a mean or angry way towards us. If anything, they were more anxious and despondent. But, they loved in the ways they knew how. My grandmother obliged to our frequent requests for back rubs. My grandfather excelled at what he called 'picking.' Always keeping their emotions at a safe distance.

When you understand them you can see why my mother struggled so much to become the loving motherly figure she so desperately wanted for herself as a child. She didn't know how . . .

Looking back now, I can see that in her attempt to obtain the motherly love that she never received as a child she unknowingly was taking it from me instead of giving it to me.

You can hear it in the language of "My babies" and "My, My, My."

You can see it in the way she grabs and squeezes instead of approaches and embraces.

You can feel it in the way she pulls within what she is without instead of expressing without what she has within.

As a hyper-sensitive child with extreme sensory acuity I often experienced the underlying intent over the surface level act. I could feel the emotional taking even though the behavior may be thought to be giving. I feel when someone is genuine. I feel authenticity. I feel when someone lies.

It's like a different language. An invisible communication of energetic intent that is felt intuitively. In *Finding YOU*, I'll break down the science behind this so you can better understand how to control your own energetic intent.

For now, take note of the importance in understanding your family history when it comes to understanding yourself. When you're able to understand the history behind how and why you came to be it allows you to make sense of who you are.

Here's an excerpt from my journal on October 9, 2023 where I uncover this connection between lack of emotional communication and my needed ability to feel things in order to understand the people around me:

> *Because I never had any communication of feelings as a child from parents or family I had to find a new way to understand how people felt. This is probably why I can 'feel things' intuitively ... I also can feel the moment when I've been successful on my 'hunt' and a girl falls for me.*

I can remember listening for the sound of my dad's tires in the driveway to determine the mood he was going to be in that day. I could tell by the way he drove, closed the door and walked up the steps how that evening would be in the house.

You can see how I had to use the data points that were shown on the surface around me to interpret the emotions of everyone underneath. The environment that I existed in forced my mind to adapt and it did.

Which is kinda beautiful when you think about it? Because of the environment I grew up in, the people I grew up with, and the way that emotion was communicated, my mind developed a new way of interpreting emotions through a variety of different data points in the environment.

This is called sensory-acuity, which you'll learn about more later on.

The Death of Wonder

Before those six words at the football banquet, I was a kid who saw the world differently. Who processed it differently. Who wasn't afraid to be himself.

After that moment it's like something fundamental started to split inside of me. It's like my psyche fractured, and part of me—the curious little boy—went into hiding.

I began to construct a version of myself designed to survive in a world that had made it clear: being myself wasn't enough. Being curious, creative, and sensitive wasn't valued. Following orders, being tough, shutting up and doing what you're told—that's what mattered.

So I adapted. I evolved. I became what the world seemed to want.

But adaptation is a tricky thing. Because what keeps you alive can also keep you from living.

Learning to Hide

The thing about killing off a part of yourself is that it doesn't happen all at once. It's not clean. You don't just wake up the next morning with a completely different personality. Death happens in stages. Slowly. Painfully. Like watching yourself fade away in a mirror that gets a little cloudier each day.

Over time the changes began to take shape. Small at first, then bigger. The curious kid who asked questions started to quiet down. The creative spark that used to light me up from the inside began to dim. I learned to read the room before I spoke.

I followed another rule in our household when adults are talking—*You don't speak unless spoken to.*

I had to watch how others acted, then interpret those actions and figure out who I should be in each moment. The anxiety started early, though I didn't have a name for it then. Always worrying about how I was behaving and how it would be interpreted by others.

My body would betray me in moments when I needed to be strong—butterflies in my stomach before football practice, a racing heart when called on in class, that familiar tightness in my chest when I felt exposed. I learned to interpret these signals as weakness, as something to overcome rather than understand.

School became a battlefield. Not just with other kids, but with myself. Between the ages of six and fifteen, I developed a pattern of not going to my first day of school. I can look back now and see it was out of fear of judgment.

I also experienced two significant emotional events during that time period that would unknowingly rock my family from the inside out. When I was in third grade my brother's best friend took his own life. I can still remember his smile and hear his laugh like it was yesterday. I'll never forget the day he died, either.

I can remember the moment my brother came downstairs and told me and my mom sitting on the couch. I can remember the grief counselor being there the next day. I can remember staying out of school for a week or so.

But, I don't remember anything after that.

If my timeline is correct then that summer or the next is when my brother, dad, and our best family friends were in a boating accident. A teenager on a jetski T-boned the boat my dad was in that was pulling my brother on waterskis. My brother was in the water and he had to swim the boy's body to the boat where my dad pulled him in.

Unfortunately, the kid died that day. When the kid hit the boat at 30 mph his head hit first. You can imagine the result. I don't know why, but I can feel their sadness writing this now. I can still remember walking up the street from the beach that day and getting the news and sprinting back to the water.

Things were different after these events . . .

My brother struggled to cope and after a time turned to alcohol as his coping strategy. This was not tolerated in my father's house and created a major conflict between my father, brother and mother.

This excerpt from my journal on September 3, 2023 shows how these events were perceived by me and how I later addressed them with my father:

> I'm reflecting on how my parents were more concerned about how others viewed them than what was actually going on with their children.
>
> The reality is that most parents live in their own stories and aren't willing to be present with their kids. They don't have real conversations with them. When my brother was in his "bad phase" of drinking and getting in trouble the biggest thing I remember my dad being upset about was how it made him look since he was in law enforcement.

When I had my first "come to jesus" talk with my dad I told him that my brother had his best friend commit suicide, pulled a dead kid out of the water in a boat accident and struggled to cope with his own anxiety, fear, guilty and emotional turmoil . . . And all you did was yell at him and punish him when he really needed a father to love him and help him through what he was dealing with.

When my therapist asked:

"What part of you changed because you went through this and watched your brother go through this? What became true for you because you lived through this with your brother and watched your dad not show up?"

My answer: The only thing that comes up on this is—I need to protect him. And we're alone.

As you can imagine, going to school was not the focus of my overactive, hypervigilant, energetically sensitive and emotionally intuitive mind. I'd make up excuses. Say I was sick. Anything to avoid walking through those doors where I knew I didn't fit in. Anything to avoid more pressure being placed on and inside of my mind.

I'd sit at home, physically fine but mentally paralyzed by the thought of all those eyes on me, all those people judging me for being. My parents didn't get it. How could they?

They'd never been inside my head. Never felt the overwhelming sensation of absorbing everyone's energy. Never felt someone else's emotions so intensely they mistook them for their own. Never experienced the different view of the world that came with being me. And I didn't have the language to be able to effectively communicate what was going on either.

My dad couldn't deal with it. He didn't have time for that kind of weakness. He would get frustrated and he and my mom would fight. So, he stormed off to work instead. Which left my mom to figure out what's wrong with *her son.*

I don't remember the details of each interaction, I just remember her telling me: "You can't miss school, you have to go."

Or him: "You better bet your ass you're going to school today, *boy."*

So eventually, I'd go. I'd force myself through those doors. But the fear never went away. It just changed form. I can remember one year my grandfather came to walk me to school because my mom had to leave. I didn't want to go, of course. He wouldn't listen to me. So, I threw up on the front doors of the school. An instant ticket back home.

It wasn't until 2023, when going through a MDMA therapy session, that a part of my Wounded Child felt safe enough to share why he was so hurt.

He asked the therapist during the session:

"Why didn't anyone ask what's wrong with me or why I was so scared? They just yelled at me to go to school."

Communicating your feelings didn't happen in my family. Unless it was anger you didn't talk about it. So, the overwhelming emotions I was experiencing got buried. The time period in junior high school was especially brutal. Missing two weeks of school gets you noticed. Not in a good way, either.

Plus, before I had big muscles and was the workout guy . . . I had man-boobs. Or at least, that's what my classmates called them.

Even though I hung out with the "cool kids," I was always the third wheel. Always a "friend" but never a "boyfriend." The girls in our group would pick on me in what they thought was an innocent way, calling me "Man Boobs."

What was innocent fun to them was absolute torture to me. With each joke, each nickname, each sidelong glance in the locker room, another piece of the real me died. Another brick was laid in the wall I was building between myself and the world. Between the parts of ME.

I started to believe the lie that every sensitive kid eventually faces: **that there was something fundamentally wrong with me.**

That I needed to change. That being me wasn't enough.

So I changed, again.

At Christmas in eighth grade, when I was thirteen, my dad got me a gym membership. This was the beginning of something new. Something that I didn't realize would become dangerous.

I discovered that physical strength could mask emotional vulnerability. Those muscles could become armor. That pain in the gym could distract from the pain in my head.

Training became my medicine for the anxiety that plagued me. When my chest felt tight with unnamed dread, I could make my muscles burn instead. When my hands shook with nervous energy, I could channel that into lifting heavier weights. The physical pain was clean, controllable—unlike the messy emotions I couldn't name or understand.

I learned to transform my sensitivity into anger, and my anger into fuel. I would sit at the gym thinking about all the negative things in my mind before every set to "amp myself up." If people could have seen inside my head during those workouts, they would have been terrified *of me.* Scratch that, they'd be terrified **for me.**

This became my pattern: take pain, turn it into anger, use that anger to fuel action. The negative side of this is that I would accomplish something that didn't give me any fulfillment. So no matter what I did, there was still a void to be filled.

The Splits Continued

My coming of age ceremonies and lessons learned came in a rapid fiery blaze that in hindsight were transformation catalysts. Unfortunately, most of the lessons I wouldn't learn until decades later.

I had just gotten over the fear of attending school and I lost the relationship with one of my closest friends. He was caught with a pipe and a small amount of marijuana in his locker at school and suspended for it. My father demanded I no longer hang out with or speak with him anymore after that. The son of a law enforcement officer couldn't be associated with that type of behavior. Little did he know, that pipe and bag of marijuana was brought to school for me.

I was terrified that my father would find out. So, what did I do? Stopped talking to my friend. In response, he took on a clear and public disliking of me. Rightfully so—I left him and never explained why. Leaving me with a dark secret and guilty conscience I would live with for twenty years before fully processing it.

That friend taught me about loyalty and I am grateful for him to this day for never telling "my secret" and ratting me out. I had much more to learn though and like I said, the lessons came faster than I'd recommend.

In tenth or eleventh grade, my best friend told me he didn't want to be friends anymore because I was "weird." I think it was more because I started dating his old girlfriend, but this was still a tough blow. Once again, I was being told that being "Ryan" was not okay.

We eventually became friends again. We were captains of the football team together. We had many positive memories together. But I never forgot that moment—walking into school one morning when my best friend told me he didn't want to be friends anymore.

It was just another confirmation of what I already believed: something was wrong with me. The real me wasn't acceptable. The only way to survive was to become someone else.

The curious, sensitive boy was gone—locked away somewhere deep inside. In his place was someone else. Someone tougher. Someone angrier. Someone who would never be hurt again.

This was the beginning of what I now understand as the Protector.

The part of me that emerged from the ashes of that first death. The part that swore it would never let anyone hurt me again—even if that meant hurting myself first.

And for a while, it worked. By twelfth grade, all those girls who had picked on me in seventh and eighth grades were either cheating on their boyfriends with me or crying because I wouldn't date them.

I had shown them. I had proven myself. I had won.

. . . That's him talking now. You can tell by his fiery arrogance.

But with each victory, the boy I used to be slipped further away. His voice grew quieter. His light dimmed. Until one day, I couldn't hear him at all.

And that's when the real trouble began.

Looking back now, I can see that first split with perfect clarity. I can trace so many of the problems in my adult life back to that moment at the football banquet. That single sentence—"Why can't you be more like that?"—did more damage than any physical blow ever could.

Words have power. Especially from the people who are supposed to love us most. When someone who should protect you instead becomes the source of your pain, it creates a wound that doesn't heal easily. Even if they didn't intend for it to do that type of damage. It creates a divide inside you that grows wider with time.

And here's what I need you to understand: If you're reading this and parts of my story feel familiar—if you've ever dimmed your light to make others comfortable, if you've ever hidden your true self behind a mask of toughness or success or indifference—you're not alone.

That split you feel inside? That disconnect between who you really are and who you pretend to be? It's not just you. And it's not your fault.

Society tells men that sensitivity is weakness. That curiosity is naivety. That feeling deeply is somehow failing. We're told to "man up," to "push through," to silence the parts of ourselves that make us human.

I believed those lies for decades. And they nearly destroyed me.

The split didn't make me stronger. It made me a stranger to myself. It created a war inside me that would rage for years. A war that would eventually force me to my knees.

But that breaking point was still years away. First, I had to build more walls. More armor. More masks.

And that's exactly what I did.

Key Insight: Sometimes a single moment can change everything. "Why can't you be more like that?" wasn't about helping me improve—it was the moment I learned that being myself wasn't enough. That little boy didn't need to change. He just needed to be seen and accepted for who he was.

Reflection Questions:

- Can you identify a moment when you first learned that parts of yourself weren't acceptable?

- What parts of yourself did you start hiding after that moment, and are you still hiding them today?

Tool Download Opportunity:
The Peak to Prison Exercise

https://www.ryanlighthouse.com/findingme

CHAPTER 2

Building the Mask of Control

Survival in my environment demanded more than just silence . . . It demanded control. Control over my body, my emotions, my environment, my future. If I could control it, I could predict it. If I could predict it, it couldn't hurt me.

It demanded a new identity.

The old me was too weird. He needed to be replaced with someone stronger. Someone tougher. Someone who wouldn't get hurt.

The environment that created my need to "feel things" intuitively had also shown me exactly what I needed to become. I knew I couldn't be me anymore. That kid was too soft. Too sensitive. I needed to be strong like Dad wanted. Invisible when necessary. Perfect in execution. Never vulnerable. Never asking for what I needed.

After watching death touch our family twice, after seeing how quickly everything could shatter, the mask wasn't just about social survival. It was about controlling a world that had proven itself unpredictable and cruel.

If I could control the perception of myself and the environment I existed in, I could be safe.

Control created predictability. If I could predict it, I could prepare for it. If I could prepare for it, it wouldn't hurt me. Eventually, I would use this control system everywhere:

- Control my body = control how others see me

- Control information = control responses

- Control emotions = control vulnerability

- Control perception = control acceptance

The Laboratory of Transformation

The gym gave me my first taste of control. Input equals output. Effort equals results. It was mathematical. Clean. Controllable. It became my sanctuary. My laboratory. The place where I could transform myself into someone new. Someone safe.

When my dad got me that gym membership, it provided me with a powerful medium for change. I started small, just trying to get rid of those man boobs that had become a source of constant torment. But something unexpected happened when I started lifting weights. Something clicked inside me.

My body responded to training quicker than expected. Soon, I was pushing harder, recovering faster, and reshaping my body. Seeing this change became addictive. For the first time in my life, I found something that made me feel powerful instead of powerless. Transforming my body was also transforming my mind.

The gym wasn't just about getting stronger. It was about eliminating vulnerability. Each pound of muscle, each reduction in body fat percentage, was another step toward the perfect exterior that would keep me safe.

In hindsight, I wasn't building a body, I was building armor. Specifically, an armor-plated chest to protect my heart. This was how I would kill off the weakness, softness and sensitivity that wasn't accepted. I was building the persona and mask of the strong silent type.

So no one could hurt me.

Side Note: *To really bring home the intense focus on discipline and perfection that infected me—Since I got that gym membership in eighth* *grade, I haven't gone more than three days without training. Any more than that and I would feel depressed and worthless.*

The same kid who couldn't face the first day of school was now building armor thick enough to face anything. This was the template and pattern that would define my teenage years. Identify any weakness or vulnerability and eliminate it through relentless perfection. Then, build impenetrable armor so it never returns.

I would apply this same approach to everything—relationships, academics, and later, business. Control and eliminate the perception or presence of any weakness.

The Three Identities

By high school, the transformation was well underway. I was no longer the kid with man boobs who got picked on. I was becoming someone else entirely.

These journal entries outline the transformation. From September 5, 2023:

I've had 3-4 distinct identities that I can think of . . .

Ryan—This was me as a young child. Probably only lasting into late elementary school.

Obie—This is the nickname of all the males on the Obernesser side of the family. Dates way back to my great great great grandfather and his 2 brothers. This identity period existed in my teens. Pretty much until I went to Buffalo.

During this time my identity was 100% tied to my body . . . because that's what I was known for. By friends, family, girls, coaches, the gym I went to etc. After coming out of a period where I was crippled with anxiety and fear of judgment this was the first time I received lots of positive praise and attention.

. . . all for my body.

I can remember explaining to someone the reason why I would never get fat or stop working out . . .

I told them it was because it's "Who I am" not "What I do."

What's interesting about that is even at that time I knew that statement was dangerous.

But here's the thing about masks: they protect you, but they also hide you—even from yourself.

The stronger I got physically, the more disconnected I became from that kid inside. The more I learned to use anger as fuel, the less I could access any other emotion. The more I built this new identity around being tough and strong, the harder it became to remember who I was before.

I started to notice other changes too. The way I spoke changed. The way I carried myself changed. Even the way I thought changed. I went from being a kid who asked "why" about everything to a teenager who didn't question anything.

This is where the Protector was locked into control. The part that said, "I'll keep you safe, no matter what. I'll make sure no one ever hurts you again." The part of me that emerged from the perception that my environment was a constant threat.

And for a while, I believed that was a good thing. I believed the Protector was saving me. I didn't understand that while I was building this mask to protect me from external threats, I was also suffocating something essential inside me. Something I wouldn't fully appreciate until it was almost too late.

By the time I was in college, the mask was firmly in place. The transformation was complete. I had built an identity that could move through the world without being hurt. An identity that could not only survive but dominate.

But it came at a cost. A cost I wouldn't understand for decades.

From my journal, September 5, 2023:

Ryan #2—This is a 2nd version of Ryan when I was in school in Buffalo. I didn't really have a set identity here . . . Probably the biggest workout, jacked asshole would be a good one. Working out was still my main identifier here.

To give you an idea of how I behaved . . . I can remember being in a 200 person lecture hall for neuro anatomy and these 2 girls were obnoxiously talking behind me. So, I kindly asked them to "please shut the fuck up so I could pay attention to the professor."

When I arrived at Buffalo I worked at Abercrombie and Fitch and my manager told my girlfriend (who also worked there) to be careful of me because I seemed like an asshole and a player. In her defense, I had already slept with ⅖ girls that worked there in my first couple months.

This was another weird period for me . . . I just became whoever I needed to be to get what I wanted and then always found myself in a bad situation when I finally stopped pretending to be someone else.

Ryan OB—This identity came about when I started getting involved in masterminds and focused 99% on business. I can actually remember consciously making the decision that I was no longer going to be the "workout guy"—I was going to be the business guy.

It's no wonder I don't know who I am. I don't think I've ever known who I was . . . I'm thinking this is because I've never been witnessed and approved of just for being ME.

Yeah, that's ME. Psychoanalyzing me.

I look back at pictures from that time now, and I barely recognize myself. Not just physically, but in the eyes. There's a hardness there. A distance. Like I'm looking at someone else entirely. I'm reminded of something someone told me once, they said: "You and your brother have the same thousand-mile stare." We do. Almost as if sometimes we're gone. And for a long time . . .

In many ways, I was.

This is the trap so many of us fall into. We adapt to survive. We build identities that protect us. We learn to play the game. And slowly, piece by piece, we lose ourselves in the process.

The mask becomes the man. The performance becomes the person. The strategy becomes the self.

Until one day, you look in the mirror and don't know who's looking back.

That's the real danger. Not that others won't see you, but that you won't recognize yourself. That you'll spend decades living as someone else. That you'll succeed at everything except being you.

I spent years perfecting this mask. Years becoming someone I thought would be safe. Years building a fortress around the wounded parts of me.

But fortresses don't just keep threats out. They keep you locked in.

While the physical transformation was obvious to everyone around me, something else was happening beneath the surface. Something more subtle. More dangerous.

I was learning to read people. To analyze them. To figure out what they wanted and become that person. I became a chameleon— changing colors depending on who I was with and what I needed from them.

In class, I learned to be invisible when I needed to. To shrink myself. To not ask the questions that burned inside me because I knew they would make me stand out.

When I did stand out, it was on my terms. On the football field. In the weight room. Places where the parts of me I was willing to show were considered strengths, not weaknesses.

The ironic part? Everyone thought I was confident. Clean cut, with muscles. Captain of the football team. Good student. Lots of friends. They had no idea that everything they saw was just a sophisticated defense mechanism. A carefully constructed mask designed to hide the wounded kid underneath.

The most frustrating part was when I started to see it but couldn't change it.

> So, if I've only ever received praise or a sense of self-worth for the external behaviors I do, accomplishments I make or way I look (aka: external identifiers / validators) . . . how will I ever find self-worth in ME?

> P.S.—The most frustrating part of this stuff is being so aware of my own shit but only seeing it hindsight and not knowing how to "fix" it or "change" it.

By the time I hit twelfth grade, I'd found a way to control my internal and external environment in a way that made me safe. Remember that best friend who told me he didn't want to be friends anymore because I was "weird"? Well, after I changed, we became close again. We were even captains of the football team together.

The girls who had commented on my "man boobs" in middle school? They were now curious about my muscles. Suddenly, I was no longer the third wheel and good "friend." There was this new experience of having girls pursuing me. I'd flipped the script completely and there was no going back.

No one would ever make me feel small again. No one would ever have power over me.

This pattern, "I'll show you," became one of the driving forces in my life.

Every rejection, every criticism, every slight became fuel for the fire. My mission was clear . . . To anyone that wronged me, doubted me, slighted me or rejected me—I would prove them all wrong.

I can remember that for a long time I kept a list. A list of everyone who doubted me. I would make them regret ever underestimating me. Each time I succeeded, each time I "showed them," the mask became stronger. More permanent. More real.

The Protector grew more confident. More aggressive. More in control.

The Brain grew sharper. More strategic. More detached.

And that original me? That curious, feeling, creative kid? He got pushed further and further into the darkness. So deep that, for a long time, I forgot he was even there.

I became obsessed with control. Control over my body. Control over my emotions. Control over how others perceived me.

The gym was perfect for this. There was a direct correlation between effort and results. Put in the work, follow the plan, and you get stronger. It was predictable. Mathematical. Safe.

The rest of life wasn't like that. The rest of life was messy and uncertain and filled with people who could hurt you. But in the gym, I was in control.

This need for control extended to every area of my life. I developed systems, routines, structures. Ways to predict outcomes. Ways to eliminate variables. Ways to ensure I always came out on top.

Every social interaction became a calculation. A strategy to avoid rejection and manipulate acceptance. If I do X, they will respond with Y. If I say this, they will think that. Humans are predictable once you understand their patterns. Their insecurities. Their needs. Map these variables, and you can navigate any situation. You can get what you want without ever being vulnerable.

The Brain wasn't emotional like the Protector. The Brain was cold. Analytical. Strategic. The Brain saw patterns others missed. Made connections others couldn't follow. The Brain could memorize entire conversations, videos, visuals. Could build anything. Could solve any problem.

Together, the Protector and the Brain became my primary operating system. They worked in tandem to keep me safe, to help me achieve, to ensure I never felt that original pain again.

But there was a cost.

The more I relied on these parts of myself, the more disconnected I became from everything else. Joy. Creativity. Wonder. Connection. All the things that make life worth living started to feel distant. Inaccessible.

There eventually would come a time where seeing my reflection in a window or a mirror, I wouldn't recognize myself. It was disorienting. Like looking at a stranger wearing my face.

The more that the parts of myself pushed me forward, the more of ME I lost. Banished into the shadows where it couldn't disrupt the system my parts had built.

The Cost of Control

By the time I was finishing high school, the mask was so complete, so convincing, that even I believed it was real. I thought this was who I was supposed to be. Who I had to be.

I was strong. I was tough. I was in control.

And no one—absolutely no one—could hurt me.

Or so I thought.

What I didn't understand then was that the very defenses I'd built to protect myself were becoming my prison. The mask I wore to survive was suffocating the parts of me that needed to breathe. The control I had built to protect me was actually limiting me.

And eventually, something would have to give.

But before that breaking point, I had to believe the mask was working. I had to prove to myself and everyone else that I'd figured it out. That I was no longer that weak, sensitive kid who believed he wasn't accepted. The kid who believed he was unlovable.

I was becoming someone new. Someone strong. Someone safe.

And I was willing to sacrifice anything—even myself—to maintain that illusion.

I spent decades perfecting this mask. Years becoming someone I thought would be safe. Years building a fortress around the wounded part of me.

I didn't realize that the very walls I built to protect myself were also keeping me prisoner.

That realization would come later. Much later. After those walls had grown so high and so thick that I couldn't even remember what freedom felt like.

But before I could break free, I had to believe the prison was a palace.

And for a while, I did.

Key Insight: The gym became my sanctuary and my prison. Control became my drug of choice. Every rep built strength and armor. The very thing that saved me also began to limit me. Sometimes our greatest strengths are born from our deepest wounds, and that's both beautiful and limiting.

Reflection Questions:

- What "armor" have you built to protect yourself, and how is it limiting you now?

- Which of your greatest strengths might actually be sophisticated defense mechanisms?

- Where in your life are you trying to control outcomes that are inherently uncontrollable?

Part Two

Hiding ME

CHAPTER 3

War Games

High school is where I perfected the *art of control* as survival.

After years of building the mask, I'd finally created a system that worked: Take pain. Turn it into fuel. Use that fuel to build armor, systems and methods of control for protection. The formula was simple and effective, even if the results were hollow.

School wasn't about learning anymore. It was about flawless execution. About proving something. About making sure nobody could ever make me feel the way I felt for all those years prior again.

When I looked around at everyone else, they seemed to be playing a different game entirely. They were making friends, finding themselves, figuring out who they wanted to be. Meanwhile, I was at war. Not just with others, but with myself.

Every achievement wasn't a celebration. It was a necessity. Every social interaction wasn't about connection. It was about perception. Every relationship wasn't about intimacy. It was about validation.

I was locked in a pattern I couldn't see. Building a fortress of perfection and control I thought was protecting me, but was actually trapping me.

The sad part? I was really fucking good at it.

The Strategic Mind

What most people never saw was what happened off the battlefield. The constant calculation. The strategic thinking. The way I analyzed every social situation like it was an environment to be controlled or a game to be won.

I became a student of human interaction, mapping others' expectations so I could meet them flawlessly. This wasn't just about social success—it was about controlling every variable so nothing unexpected could hurt me. The real me remained hidden, protected behind a perfect performance of whatever persona was required.

I learned to model outcomes mentally. To predict how people would react. To manipulate situations to my advantage. Then, manipulate myself to match those situations. It wasn't something I did consciously at first. It was just survival. But over time, it became second nature.

I could walk into a party and within seconds catalog everyone's expectations. Who needed to be impressed. Who might see through my performance. Who could accept or reject me. I'd map the entire social landscape in my mind, then craft the perfect adaptation for each interaction.

I became a chameleon, intuitively sensing what each person needed me to be and becoming that version of myself flawlessly. With the football team, I embodied the perfect teammate they respected. With girls, I presented the perfect balance of mystery and confidence they found attractive. With teachers, I was the perfect student with untapped potential who just needed to "apply himself."

None of it was entirely false. But none of it was authentically me either. They were all fragments of myself. Carefully curated, perfectly performed aspects that I'd learned to deploy in the right contexts at the right times.

I don't think anyone ever saw all the versions. No single person knew the complete picture. Because there wasn't a whole me anymore. I'd fragmented myself into specialized parts that I could perfect for each situation where rejection threatened.

The Protector perfected the physical image, the confrontations, the appearance of invulnerability.

The Brain perfected the strategic calculations, the social predictions, the pattern recognition that kept me one step ahead of potential rejection.

And the original me? That curious, sensitive boy? He was locked away somewhere so deep I couldn't hear him anymore. An acceptable sacrifice for the perfect safety I was constructing.

By senior year, this perfect adaptation had achieved its aim—at least externally. Captain of the football team. Socially validated. Pursued by the same girls who had once rejected me.

I'd engineered the perfect transformation.

But perfection is its own kind of prison. Once you achieve it, you have to maintain it. You have to keep performing flawlessly, keep meeting every expectation, keep anticipating every potential criticism—because the moment your perfection slips, rejection feels inevitable.

So I kept refining. Kept performing. Kept curating my image, my body, my social value.

The emptiness didn't matter. The exhaustion didn't matter. The disconnect didn't matter.

All that mattered was being accepted.

Because in my mind, only perfection would result in acceptance and could protect me from the pain of rejection.

I had no idea I was pursuing an impossible standard. That the more perfectly I performed these external roles, the further I moved from the imperfect authenticity that might have actually brought connection.

I was perfecting the performance. But I was losing myself in the process.

By the time I was finishing high school, I had turned strategic thinking into an art form. What began as defense mechanisms—ways to navigate the social battlefield of adolescence—had evolved into sophisticated cognitive tools. Tools that would stay with me long after graduation.

Building Mental Models

These mental models I'd built in high school didn't disappear as I grew older. They became more refined, more powerful. The ability to read rooms, analyze threats, and strategize constantly became second nature—skills that would save me more than once in the years to come.

From my journal, June 1, 2023:

> I have this weird ability to build models in my head to solve problems and map out scenarios. It only happens on certain occasions. It's like accessing a certain area of my mind that's not always open for me. When you said I am at 40% it got me thinking about this.

In 2017, these same mental patterns would save me from what could have been a dangerous situation in Germany. What's striking is how automatically my brain slipped into the same strategic mode I'd perfected in high school, only now with higher stakes.

Here's what happened:

My brother and I were at Oktoberfest. We made the mistake of going directly from the plane to the party at 8 AM after taking a red eye. Exhausted but excited, we dropped our bags at the hotel front desk, changed clothes in the bathroom stall, sprayed on some cologne, and took off for the festival. We were having a blast drinking, making new friends, and loving everything about Germany.

We partied pretty hard and made friends with some guys from Denmark. All was good until it wasn't. One of our new Denmark friends returned from the bathroom, sat next to me and whispered in my ear, "Are you friends with these people?" as he motioned to the couple across the table.

"No, we just met," I told him.

"Good, because the guy has been very rude to my friend and my friend is going to fuck him up right now. Watch."

Something wasn't right. The guy he was referring to had been nothing but nice to everyone. If something doesn't fit, if you feel like it just doesn't belong, that's a red flag. A radically increased level of aggression against an innocent bystander is a red flag.

I turned to my brother and whispered, "We need to leave. I'll meet you at the clocktower."

I began to stand and told my Danish friend that I had to go to the bathroom.

He had different plans and said, "No, you stay with me."

Let's just say that I don't do well with being told what to do, so I grabbed my brother and stood anyway to go to the bathroom.

Mr. Denmark stood too. His bigger, much scarier friend stood with him.

"We're coming with you," he said. Then, grabbed me by the elbow and proceeded to escort us to the bathroom.

At this point, my brother was freaking out and starting to argue with the guy.

I don't know how, but on that walk to the bathroom being escorted by these two Danish guys, despite being exhausted, despite being in a foreign country, despite the alcohol, I was able to identify a rendezvous landmark, map out in my head a scenario with a choke point and opportunity, and formulate an escape plan in seconds.

After the bathroom, I knew we needed more chaos—more opportunity. So I suggested we get more beer. If we got more beer then we'd have to go to the serving area, which meant more chaos. More chaos meant more opportunity for escape.

We got to the serving area and grabbed a high top. The server came back after taking our order and asked for payment.

"Sorry, I don't have any cash," I said as I squeezed my brother's hand.

He said, "Yeah, me neither."

That left Mr. Denmark, who was out of cash too.

The server said that someone needed to pay for the beer or we would be kicked out.

Mr. Denmark told me to go to the ATM. "Sorry, I only had cash," I replied, shrugging.

My brother said the same thing.

"Ugh. Fine. You two don't move and I'll be right back," said Mr. Denmark as he stomped away.

As soon as he was out of sight, we ran to the nearest exit. Sprinting through Oktoberfest as fast as we could, slamming into people, stomping through puddles, headed straight for the gate I'd mentally marked earlier.

That's the fastest we ever ran.

It's scary to think about. In that moment of danger, all the strategic pathways I had built through my childhood and beyond lit up like a Christmas tree. My brain didn't have to think. It already knew how to find the escape route, how to create a distraction, how to exploit a weakness, how to navigate the chaos to get us to safety.

This is what the Protector and the Brain had been built for. The ultimate survival mechanism, forged through years of navigating social minefields, now deployed in a real-life threat scenario.

Looking back at that moment in Oktoberfest, I recognize the same patterns I'd developed as a teenager. The constant assessment of social dynamics. The quick identification of threats. The strategic planning of escape routes. The manipulation of situations to my advantage.

What had begun as a way to survive in childhood had become so deeply ingrained that it functioned even when my conscious mind was impaired by alcohol and sleep deprivation.

The Survival Algorithm

This is how deeply these patterns become embedded. They don't just help you navigate difficult periods of your life—they become the operating system that **runs your entire life**. For better and worse.

Because while these skills had saved me at Oktoberfest, the same hypervigilance, the same constant calculation, the same strategic detachment, continued to keep me separated from authentic connection. From vulnerability. From myself.

I was controlling every outcome. I was maintaining perfect predictability. I thought I was safe.

But I was still at war.

Key Insight: I learned to treat life like a chess game where I needed to control every piece. When you're always ten moves ahead, nothing can surprise you. Nothing can hurt you. But you also can't truly live in the present moment . . .

Reflection Questions:

- Where do you find yourself trying to control situations or people when you could be trusting the process?

- What might open up if you approached situations with curiosity instead of strategy?

CHAPTER 4

The Foundation Crumbles

The Cracks Begin to Show

The war in my mind and illusion of control continued as I navigated the college years . . .

Originally, I was enrolled at Springfield College and was set to play football. Then, a few months before the summer training camp began, the war in my mind boiled over.

The same fears and anxiety that I felt every year before school as a child were returning. I began questioning my desire to go to Springfield, my ability to play football after getting injured and my confidence to experience a new environment on my own. A change like this meant I had to temporarily sacrifice control. Of course, there was a girl involved too.

Here's how I described it in my journal, May 23, 2023:

> *Shortly after making the decision to stay home and not go to Springfield I discovered that the girl I stayed for was 'cheating on me'. I can remember dropping her off at her house after going on vacation. I was looking in the rearview mirror as I drove away and watched her run across the street to her neighbor's house who was her 'friend'. I don't know about you. But, I've never run to see my neighbor after returning from a week long vacation with my boyfriend and his family.*
>
> *When I attempted to discuss this situation with my dad and get advice he decided that was the best time to tell me a story that shattered my view of him.*

My mom and Dad met working together in a restaurant. My mom got pregnant and so they were going to get married. Before the wedding, my mom found my dad in bed with another woman at my Grandma's house. A child out of wedlock is unacceptable in my grandparents eyes so they told him he had to make it right. My parents were married the following week in a courthouse with no one there except parents.

Apparently, this was his way of telling me I should forgive the girl who cheated on me because my mom forgave him.

I saw this as the Father I was supposed to trust defending someone who hurt me. Once again, rejecting the emotions and needs of Ryan.

So, with a few weeks left of summer before I shipped off to training camp I called the coach and backed out. I don't remember any specifics of this event other than my parents and the coach being disappointed and angry with my decision.

There wasn't any time to process this so I did what I did best—buried the anger, sadness, and hurt. Then, used it as fuel to drive myself harder. At community college, the more the anger filled me and the deeper I buried the sadness, the more confident I became. On the outside at least. I dumped the girl, started partying with my brother's friends and decided that if this time period of my life was too difficult, I'd skip it. So, I grew up.

At nineteen, I was done with the frat parties and basement hangouts. Actually, I never really was into them to begin with if I'm honest. I approached college life differently . . . I was going to upscale restaurants, nightclubs and bars with my brother's (read: my) new friends. They were entrepreneurs with money. They accepted me and always took care of me like a little brother. They showed me how to utilize the tools of money and success to further take control of a situation. Two tools I would quickly find myself without when I graduated and moved away.

After I graduated from community college, I transferred to University of Buffalo to complete my bachelor's in Exercise Science. On the day I arrived at the school for my orientation something interesting happened. I was informed that some of my credits were not eligible for the program and I was missing one course. Unfortunately, that course wasn't offered until the spring so I couldn't be admitted to the program.

To this day, I have no idea how we got that far into the process before anyone notified me of this. As a result I had to decide to either withdraw from school or take up a second major and sign up for the course in the spring.

I decided to take up Psychology as a second major and stacked my semester that year so I could graduate on time with two degrees. While it was a quick remedy, it wasn't at all what I had planned.

This surprise change threw me right back into being that terrified child who was afraid to go to school the first day. All of the confidence that I had manufactured over the last two years pretending to be a certain version of me disappeared as soon as that version no longer applied to the situation.

I quickly found myself back in the darkness of my mind fighting the war I thought I had won, again. The darkness, anger and sadness continued to consume me. My best friend, David, reminded me recently of the text messages I used to send him saying "I need you."

At the time, he didn't know what I meant. He does now.

All of this culminated in a moment that broke apart the final pieces of my foundation . . .

The Call That Changed Everything

I don't remember the exact moment I got the call from my mom. I imagine she was crying. What I do remember is the story she told me.

About how she thought he was having an affair.

This went on for some time, these calls from my mom. Her confiding in me. Telling me her suspicions. Putting me in the middle of something no kid—even a college-aged one—should be in the middle of.

I was away at school when all this started. Building a new life. Creating distance from the previous versions of me. Trying to establish myself as someone new, someone who wasn't defined by his past.

And then this pulled me right back into it all.

When I came home for break during this period, my dad showed up at a restaurant where me, my brother, and my best friend were eating. He decided to sit in our booth and bring up this issue about him and my mom in front of my friend.

It was in this conversation that I gave him the opportunity to tell the truth.

I didn't want the details of what he may or may not have done. I asked him a very simple question about his feelings for this woman.

He lied. Remember, with the Protector and Brain working together I'm a human lie detector. I don't hear your words, I see your thoughts.

Like having the wind taken out of your sails, my respect for my father was washed away. In the mind of the Protector, this was a mortal sin. Betrayal.

Being caught in the midst of my parents' broken marriage made trust feel like a lie. It wasn't just my childhood that died—it was my belief that anyone could be safe.

If I couldn't trust my own father—the man who was supposed to protect me, guide me, show me how to be a man—then who could I trust?

No one. That was the answer that crystallized in my mind. No one.

Learning to Guard My Heart

This betrayal changed things. My relationship with my father was never the same after that moment.

The fortress I'd built to protect myself from peers and social rejection now had to protect me from something much closer. Something that should have been safe. My own family.

I began to trust people less. I became more guarded, more calculated in my relationships.

My parents didn't split up. They stayed in this weird limbo—together but broken. My mom would call me, upset about something he did. She'd confide in me things a son probably shouldn't hear about his parents' marriage. I found myself in the middle, trying to protect her while dealing with my own feelings about the whole situation.

I wanted distance from all of it. College became my escape. I threw myself into anything that would keep my mind occupied and keep me away from home. I trained in the gym harder and continued to bury the emotional pain.

I was building more walls, creating more distance between myself and anyone who might hurt me. Not in some dramatic, movie-villain way. Just in the quiet, everyday decisions to keep people at arm's length. To rely on myself instead of others. To protect the parts of me that were still vulnerable. I learned to take care of my needs first.

I didn't realize then that those same walls that kept others out were also keeping me trapped inside.

Key Insight: When trust is broken by those who should protect us, it reshapes how we see the world. My father's betrayal taught me that even the safest relationships could become dangerous. Learning to trust again became one of my greatest challenges and most important healing journeys.

Reflection Questions:

- What foundational beliefs about trust and safety were shattered in your formative years?

- How have these early betrayals shaped your adult relationships and business decisions?

CHAPTER 5

Crashing Down

I thought I had it all figured out. I'd built my fortress. I'd created my systems. I'd learned how to control perception with perfection. But when the final pieces of the foundation of my family crumbled, everything else started to collapse too.

The next few years were a slow-motion train wreck. I was trying to build a new life in college while the old one was falling apart back home. I was trying to create distance from my past without being pulled back into my parents' drama.

The Birthday Breakdown

My next major crash came during my birthday trip to Florida in 2010. My girlfriend and I had decided we would move south after college. We were thinking of South Carolina. So, for my birthday, we went to Florida with her family, planning to drive to SC afterward to look for apartments.

Remember how I said I'd become the alpha asshole? Well, we got into a big fight on my birthday. That night at dinner, I got drunk and was a dick to everyone. After dinner, my girlfriend told me she didn't want to go look at apartments in South Carolina anymore. I knew what that really meant. She didn't want to build a future with me. She saw my "true colors" that weekend and those weren't accepted.

At least, that's how I interpreted it in my mind.

So, it was time to run away to safety.

I waited until everyone fell asleep that night. I called a taxi and went to the airport. Hopped on a plane and never looked back. I'll never forget calling my mom as I sat in the airport in the wee hours of the morning, unable to speak. Uncontrollably crying in the middle of the airport isn't a good look.

I flew home that night, drove to Buffalo the next day, and moved everything back to Utica with my brother. I even took the cat we shared. I've never spoken to that girl since that night on my twenty-third birthday in Florida.

Here I was at home, alone, with a father I no longer respected and a mother I felt the need to protect. Everything I'd built—my relationship, my plans for the future, my identity as someone who had his shit together—it was all falling apart.

While at the time that experience crushed me, this turned out to be one of the best birthday presents I had ever received—**it was the wake up call that I needed.** I just didn't know it yet. Today, I'm grateful for it.

Moving Backwards

This wasn't just a setback. It was a complete collapse. I wasn't moving forward anymore. I was moving backward.

All that work. All that effort. All those walls and systems and strategies I'd created—and here I was, right back where I started. Living at home. Alone. Lost.

It was the first time I had to confront the possibility that my entire approach to life might be flawed. That control or being perfect might not be enough. I might never be good enough. That the fortress I'd built might not actually be protecting me at all.

But I wasn't ready to face that yet. Instead, I did what I'd always done when hurt: I adapted. I evolved. I built a new version of armor to protect myself. It would be years before I understood that I wasn't solving the problem. I was just building a bigger, more sophisticated prison.

The Final Pieces Fall

My life had become a scramble to pick up the pieces. After moving back home with my parents, the situation only got worse.

My mom decided she needed to have a cat too, since I had brought home the cat my ex-girlfriend and I had shared. She adopted one that had feline intraperitoneal disease, which passed to my cat. My cat died from it within a few months of moving home, at only one year old.

Unintentional of course, but it hurt deeply. Almost as if it was a final piece of a version of me dying with it.

Prior to breaking down in 2023, this was the last time I remember crying. Sometime around fall of 2011. My emotions turned off after this. After everything that had happened with my dad and now my mom indirectly killing my cat, I moved out. I couldn't take being in that house anymore.

I had finished up school with no clue what to do next. A psychology degree that wouldn't get me anywhere. An internal and external battle with my father. No clear path forward. Just a deep sense that I had to get away from everything and everyone I knew.

The worst part wasn't just that I'd lost my girlfriend, my plans for the future, my cat. I'd lost momentum. I'd lost direction. The strategies that had worked for me in high school—the fortress I'd built, the systems I'd created — they weren't working anymore.

The tools that had served me so well were suddenly useless. And I had no others.

This is what happens when you build your entire identity around a facade, around power and control, around never being vulnerable. When you finally encounter something you can't beat through sheer force of will or strategic thinking, you're left with nothing. No backup plan. No softer skills to fall back on. No capacity to process emotions in a healthy way.

I was numb. Angry. Lost. I couldn't see a way forward that made any sense.

But like all things, this phase didn't last forever. Eventually, I found new armor. New ways to win. New identities to construct.

I would rebuild. Stronger this time. More sophisticated. More successful. More control.

I just didn't realize I was building the same prison with fancier walls.

The next chapter of my life was about to begin. One where I would try to escape my pain through achievement, through business, and discover a woman who somehow saw through my walls.

I was still alone. Still carrying all that anger and hurt from my father's betrayal, from feeling like everyone I trusted eventually let me down.

I didn't know it then, but I was about to meet someone who would change everything.

Key Insight: Sometimes we have to lose our footing to realize we were standing on shaky ground. What felt like failure was actually my system's way of saying "this path isn't serving you anymore." The crash became the foundation for building something real.

Reflection Questions:

- What patterns in your life keep leading to the same crashes or conflicts?

- What if your setbacks are actually course corrections guiding you toward something more authentic?

CHAPTER 6

New Armor

July 2011. One month after the Florida disaster, I found myself drunk in my parents' basement wallowing in self-pity. (That's what adult men are taught to do with their emotional pain, *isn't it?* Sedate. Disconnect. Bury it. Be strong)

I had returned home and fell deep into a dark hole. For weeks I did nothing but get drunk, get high and blame the world for my problems. I refused to leave the house. I didn't want to talk to anyone.

But, on that July evening in 2011, I'm glad my friend was able to change my mind . . .

Meeting My Anchor

My friend asked me what would make me feel better, I jokingly said seeing the girl I'd had a fling with throughout high school. The one who got away, type of fling. With that as the goal, they convinced me to go to the bars that night (*I didn't even know where she lived at the time*).

But, after closing down the bars that night she was nowhere in sight. Then, as if I manifested it . . . who did I see stumbling down the middle of the street at the end of the night? That girl. I was the one stumbling— not her.

I managed to ask her out on a date for the next day to go jetskiing. I told her I would pick her up at 11:08 the next morning. By the look on her face you could tell she didn't believe me. I pulled into her driveway the next day at 11:08 AM.

We've been together ever since.

We opened a business three years later, got married in 2019 and had our first child in 2024 after two miscarriages (. . . *more on all of that later*).

Her name is Christina and she entered my life when I needed something to anchor me. After the Florida break-up, I was back home, depressed, disconnected, with a psychology degree that wouldn't get me anywhere and no clear path forward. I was totally lost.

Meeting her changed things.

Christina was different from anyone I'd met before. She had this mysterious, sexy and confident essence about her. As if she didn't care what anyone else was doing. She was in her own world. This always attracted me to her.

For the first time, I didn't deploy my chameleon abilities. I didn't become whoever I thought she needed me to be.

Something about her presence made pretending feel impossible. She saw through the performances to something authentic underneath. As if she could see the version of me I wasn't even sure existed anymore.

I didn't have to "try," I could just "be."

For the first time in my life I was connecting with someone who I felt fully accepted and unconditionally loved—ME.

That summer we spent every waking moment together. We were both figuring out the next chapter of life and were equally as lost. I was grateful to be found.

With her support, I started to find my way again. I needed a new direction. A new identity. A new way to win after so many losses. A new way to gain control of a life that had become chaos. She became someone I could actually connect with. Not completely—I wasn't capable of that yet—but more than with anyone else.

My Loyal Friend

The last time I needed saving, the iron saved me. After returning home I was in need of saving again. So, I turned to my loyal friend. The only one that never let me down. The iron of the gym.

I knew fitness. I'd been obsessed with training since my dad got me that gym membership. It was something I was good at, something I understood, something that had always given me a sense of control.

It's what allowed me to transform and I needed to transform again.

I got certified as a personal trainer and started working at the same gym that was my home as a teen. The owner, Al Calogero, was kind enough to allow me to get my start there. He took me under his wing in his own way and allowed me to learn. It wasn't a glamorous start. It wasn't particularly lucrative. But it was movement forward in a new direction.

What I discovered quickly was that my sensory acuity abilities, which I developed for protection as a child, translated beautifully into coaching. I could see patterns in movement that others missed. I could connect with clients in a way that motivated them. I could get results where others had failed.

This was something I could be good at. Something I could potentially master. Something I could use to help others. I had found a drive and purpose again.

So I went all in. I studied everything I could get my hands on. I attended seminars. I sought out mentors. I became obsessed with becoming the best coach I could be.

The results started to show . . . My client list grew. My reputation spread. I started to build a name for myself in the local athletics scene.

But working in someone else's gym had limitations. I was capped in what I could earn. I was restricted in how I could train. The equipment we had to use. I had to follow someone else's rules, someone else's system, someone else's vision.

I was under someone else's control . . . A place that I am not able to stay in. I knew if I wanted to truly succeed, if I truly wanted to be in control of my future, I needed to build something of my own.

My personal training business grew steadily. Each client was a small victory, proof that I could create value, that I had something to offer. The iron had saved me, and now I was helping others find their own salvation in the weight room.

For the next two years, I lived in the space between vision and execution, between dreaming and building. Until the right time came . . .

Business Partners

I've never been one to follow the status quo or typical way of doing things. So why would business be any different?

My personal training business was growing. Christina had started personal training herself at a different studio. Her mom suggested, *"Why don't you guys team up?"*

That's exactly what we did.

Before getting married. Before getting engaged. Before moving in together. We went into business together.

We joined forces at O.B. Training and started to take this personal training business more seriously. Our continuing education focus shifted from science to sales and from muscles to marketing. We started to see the opportunities that were in front of us.

We were a perfect team. Christina brought creativity, connection and compassion. She could make anyone feel seen and capable of more than they believed. I brought the brains of the business, systems and intensity in training. Turning the progress into measurable results.

Where I pushed, she nurtured. Where she flowed, I structured. She helped me open the lighter sides of myself that were hidden away. Her presence softened my armor. Bringing out the best of me.

Together, we created something neither of us could have built alone: **a training experience that was both transformative and sustainable.**

As our momentum picked up, so did our exposure. We attended health expos. Hosted youth speed camps and free workshops. I started presenting to some of the local sports teams.

Looking back, we were preparing for the moment we didn't know was about to happen.

The Moment

I didn't really have a concrete plan to open a gym until June 2013, when Christina and I attended our first Perform Better Summit. The legendary Thomas Plummer was speaking about the business of fitness in the first session of the morning.

As always, he brought the fire.

Over the course of ninety minutes, Thom completely shattered and rebuilt my mindset on what it meant to be a business owner. He was speaking to the older trainers in the room. The guys and gals in their late forties, fifties, some even in their sixties. I don't remember his exact words, but he asked a question that changed everything:

"At what age are you going to stop trading your hours for dollars?"

Prior to that session, I was a personal trainer who maybe wanted to open a gym. After that session, my mission crystallized:

Become a business owner who built a team to run the gym.

I decided at that moment that NOW was going to be the age I stopped trading time for money. Christina and I looked around the room and saw tired trainers looking to be saved. We decided then and there that it wouldn't be us.

When I got home from the event, I immediately began working on my business plan for O.B. Training. Every night after training clients, I'd come home and work on spreadsheets, financial projections, equipment lists, marketing strategies.

During the day I would share my ideas with clients to get feedback. My clients that were in business themselves were generous enough to offer their insights. Every night was spent building. Every day was spent refining.

Christina was there through all of it. Supporting me. Believing in me. Helping in whatever ways she could. We became a team, not just as a couple but in business. She understood the vision and was always there for support.

Over the next few months, everything accelerated. We found a location—a 5,000 square foot warehouse that had been sitting empty. We scraped together every dollar we had. Borrowed from anyone who would lend.

We were about to build something from nothing. Create a business that would either validate everything I believed about myself or destroy what little stability I'd managed to create.

I thought I was building a gym. I didn't realize I was building another fortress. One made of business metrics and revenue goals and professional achievements instead of muscle and anger and academic success.

But that revelation would come later. In that moment, all I knew was that I was finally taking action. Finally moving from dreaming to doing.

Finally creating something that was entirely mine. We set off on *"one last vacation"* as we called it and took a nine-day cruise before returning home to begin construction on our new adventure.

The next chapter of my life was about to begin—one where I would discover that building a successful business and building a successful life are two very different things.

But I didn't know that yet.

Key Insight: *Success* became my new form of protection. Business, money, achievement—these were more sophisticated ways of staying safe while still engaging with the world. But I learned that external success can't heal internal disconnection. They're different kinds of work entirely.

Reflection Questions:

- How much of your drive for success comes from authentic desire versus a need to prove something?

- How much of your identity is tied to what you do versus who you are?

Part Three

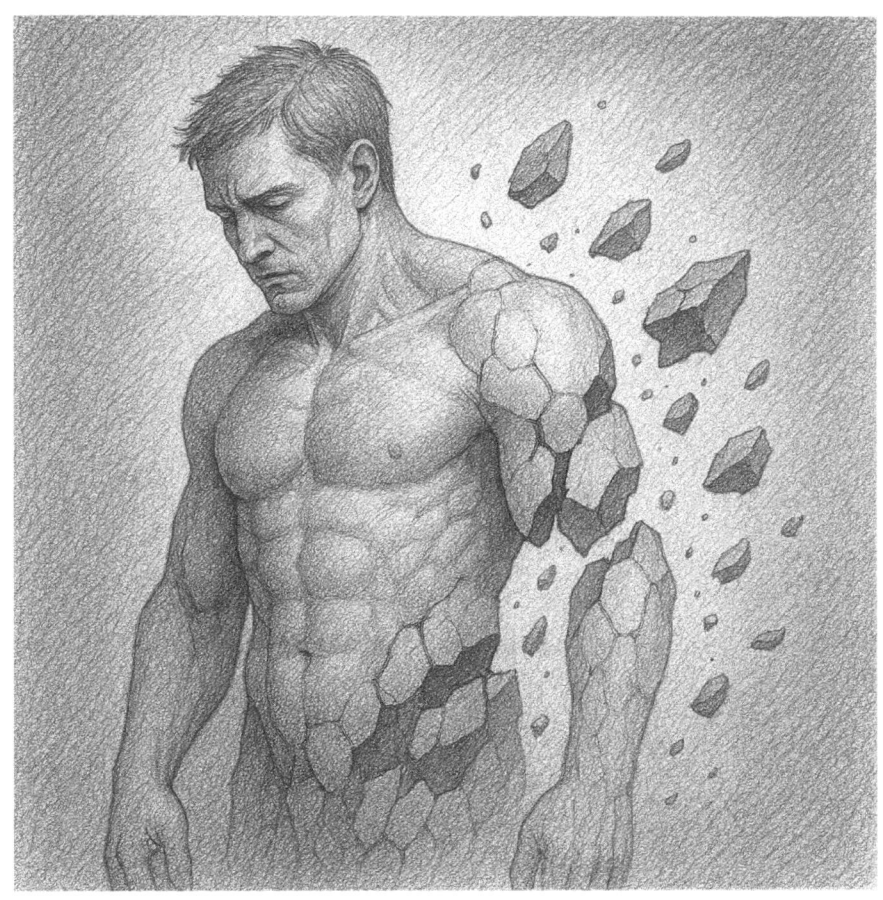

Breaking ME

CHAPTER 7

Building the Business Fortress

After re-connecting with Christina in 2011, my life began to stabilize around something real. She became my anchor while I searched for direction with a psychology degree that led nowhere practical.

Personal training became my lifeline—the one thing I understood, the one place where transformation made sense to me.

Opening a gym was terrifying and exhilarating. After three years of building my reputation as a personal trainer, of saving every dollar, of refining my vision, Christina and I were finally ready to take the leap.

When Christina and I opened our gym, the vision was crystal clear: **create a sports performance facility for youth athletes**.

I wanted to build what I never had as a kid—a place where young athletes could develop both physical and mental strength, where curiosity and questions were welcomed, where being different was an asset, not a liability.

I threw everything into it. Every dollar. Every hour. Every ounce of energy. The early days were a grind. Long hours. No money. Constant stress. But also exhilarating.

For the first time in my life, I was building something that was truly mine. Something I believed in. Something I controlled.

And surprisingly, I was good at it. Not just the training part, but the business part too. I could analyze markets and metrics, spot opportunities, devise strategies. With my emotions turned off and a mountain of anger to stand on I could push through fatigue, overcome setbacks, and I refused to quit. The only way to lose is to quit. As long as you don't stop you will never lose. This is the language that guided me. Use your armor to push through every hit, every roadblock, lost relationship, negative review, and upset client. It all reflected off of me like sunrays off a mirror's surface.

Together, the parts of ME made me navigate the rollercoaster journey of entrepreneurship with a blank stone cold face.

Reality Hits (2015-2016)

Reality has a way of testing even the best visions. Our first summer was a wake-up call—when kids went back to school, we lost 50% of our revenue overnight. The sports performance model that had worked beautifully for three months crumbled when September arrived.

We faced a brutal choice: adapt or close.

My mentor at the time put it bluntly: "The adult programs pay the bills and the sports performance is the icing on the cake."

So we adapted. We created programs for adults. We marketed to a different demographic. We became what we needed to become to survive.

And it worked. The business grew. Money started coming in. Our membership expanded. We hired coaches. We moved to a bigger facility.

From the outside, it looked like I was "living the dream" as they say. New car. New house. Growing business. Beautiful girlfriend who believed in the vision.

But something was happening beneath the surface. Each pivot away from the original vision felt like a small betrayal of that kid who just wanted to help young athletes. The kid who just wanted to help himself. Each adult program we added was another brick in a different kind of fortress—one built on compromise rather than conviction.

The Wrong Vision (2017)

By 2017, three years after opening, I woke up one morning and realized I'd built exactly what I never wanted.

The business was thriving. Money was flowing. From the outside, we were the success story everyone pointed to. *"Look at what they built in just three years."*

But walking through those doors each morning, I was surrounded by adults doing burpees instead of athletes pursuing excellence. The money was better this way. The business model more stable. The success was more impressive on paper.

It was a perfect execution of the wrong vision.

The anger was constant. I was angry at myself for not sticking to my vision. I was angry at myself for the original plan "not working." I was angry at myself for not doing what I loved to do every day.

But anger needs a target. And I had blamed myself for enough problems in my life at that point. So I turned my rage outward. I resented my clients—the very people whose loyalty kept the business alive. Even though I was the one who created the marketing to attract them, designed the programs, and sold them into joining my gym, I blamed them for me not having what I wanted.

I was so blinded by anger that I couldn't see the truth: those adults I resented had kids. Kids who wanted to train. All I had to do was ask.

When my mentor called me out on my shit, everything shifted. We invited the parents' kids to train, and suddenly we had the largest sports performance program our area had ever seen.

The vision wasn't dead—it had just taken a different path to get there.

The Best Friend Betrayal (2017)

That same year, as our business continued to grow, we decided to expand our facility. Forcing me to face another test of the patterns that had controlled my life.

I hired my best friend to handle the construction of our expansion. He'd helped with the original build. His father was both my landlord and my dad's best friend. It should have been perfect—mixing business with the people I trusted most.

But my friend had a pattern of taking on too much. He was simply spread too thin. After weeks of delays past the intended start date, with our business growth hanging in the balance, I had to make a choice.

For once, I tried to handle it differently. No anger. No aggression. Just calm, clear communication.

We went to dinner and I calmly expressed how his actions have negatively impacted my business and that I didn't want our friendship to be affected. I was going to hire someone else. This was a big step for me trying to communicate my emotions in a non-destructive way.

I thought I'd finally learned to navigate conflict without overwhelming rage.

But it didn't matter.

My friend saw betrayal where I saw boundaries. My mom came to my work and flipped out, asking "Who do you think you are?" in a tone that transported me right back to that survival environment of my childhood where I felt rejected.

When I finally stood up for myself, my parents saw an "asshole big shot" who didn't care about his friends.

I can remember being so angry that I thought I was going to cry as I ferociously yelled at her about how fucked up it was that she and my dad were running to defend my friend instead of their own son.

I can still see the terror in her eyes as she watched her son release decades of rage.

Once again, when I tried to stand up for myself—even calmly, even "correctly"—my own family chose someone else's side.

The message was clear: **my needs, my business, my boundaries didn't matter as much as keeping everyone else comfortable.**

In the end, I lost my best friend and separated myself from the "crabs" even more. Further confirmation that connection led to betrayal, that trusting others led to abandonment, that I was safer alone in my fortress.

Finding Rhythm (2018-2019)

Despite the betrayals, despite the compromises, something beautiful emerged from the chaos.

By 2018, we'd found our rhythm. The adult programs funded the youth programs I actually wanted to run. The business model that had felt like betrayal became the vehicle for the original vision.

I hired Bedros Keuilian as a business coach, investing in high-level mentorship to take things to the next level. We hit our highest revenue ever. I finally removed myself from day-to-day operations, building systems that could run without me. I was moving closer to the vision that I had seen for my future in my mind.

August 2019 was the peak. I had just married Christina—the girl I'd been chasing since I was fifteen years old. Our gym business hit an all-time high. I launched my coaching business for other gym owners. From the outside, I had achieved everything I'd worked toward.

Multiple revenue streams. Systems in place. Team handling the operations. Strategic positioning in the market. I had *everything a successful entrepreneur should want*. I had everything *I said I wanted*.

But inside? I was running on empty. I was losing control. Each achievement felt hollow. Each milestone passed without joy. Each success only highlighted the growing disconnect between who I was becoming and who I really was underneath all the armor.

I'd built a business that made money while slowly killing my soul. I'd created success that looked impressive on paper while feeling empty in my chest. I'd assembled all the pieces of entrepreneurial achieve-ment while losing the pieces of myself. Although, I didn't know it yet.

I had no idea that everything I'd built was about to be tested in ways I never imagined. That the very success I'd created would become the weight that would finally break me. That sometimes, reaching the peak is just the beginning of the fall.

But first would come 2020. And with it, a test that would push every part of me—every strategy, every defense, every carefully constructed wall—to its absolute limit.

Key Insight: What starts as a vision of service can become a prison of compromise when we prioritize survival over purpose. I built exactly what I never wanted because I was still operating from fear rather than authentic desire. Success without alignment is just a prettier cage.

Reflection Questions:

- Where have you compromised your original vision in the name of "practical" success?

- What would your career or business look like if it was built from joy rather than fear?

- How might your resentment toward your current reality be pointing you back to your true purpose?

CHAPTER 8
The Gauntlet

February, 2020 . . .

Covid hit and crushed the fitness world.

Businesses were forced to close their doors and gyms were attacked in the name of safety. We didn't miss a beat. We took our programs online within twenty-four hours of the closure announcement.

Then, over the next two months we recorded over seventy episodes of our live workout show "O.B. TV," hosted a dozen charity events and a half dozen virtual concerts to support local artists.

If I'm being honest, I like war. When things get harder, I get better. I want the pressure of survival, it feels like home. When the weak fall, I rise.

So in the beginning of Covid, we crushed it. Launched online within days. Kept all our staff employed. We expanded while the rest contracted. I was in my element—problem-solving, adapting, dominating when others were retreating.

Eight weeks of carrying the team on your shoulders is manageable. Eight months of it wears you down.

By the end of 2020, I was burnt out, miserable, and resentful of everyone who attacked us for our choice of **Freedom** and those I'd "*saved*" who never seemed to appreciate the sacrifice. The very people I'd fought to protect became the source of my frustration.

In my mind, I had sacrificed everything for them, and they barely noticed.

The Cracks Begin to Show

Since childhood my dream had always been to move south.

The ultimate goal of my gym was to be a launchpad into coaching, speaking, writing, and moving the fuck out of Utica, NY. In 2019, I was millimeters from achieving this. The fallout of 2020 put me back miles away from the goal.

In an attempt to "leap," Christina and I rented a house in St. Pete Beach from December 2020 to February 2021. A test run for the life we wanted.

Upon returning to our home in Utica, we walked into disaster. A frozen pipe had burst in the ceiling, destroying the first floor and basement. The water ran for days and the moisture in the house destroyed the upstairs as well. Our whole house needed to be gutted and rebuilt.

This was the last thing I wanted to deal with. Another problem to solve. Another distraction keeping me from my goals. If I had it my way at the time, I would have gotten back in the car and drove back to Florida leaving the house as is . . .

We were displaced for an entire year, living with Christina's parents for over six months.

It was a strange experience for me because their family dynamic is 100% the opposite of mine.

Like, they actually want to hang out with each other. That concept was completely foreign to me and unfortunately shined a bright light on the family dynamic I "could have had" or "missed out on" in my house.

I found myself lying awake on the couch at night thinking to myself, *"Why couldn't my family be like this? Why did love always feel so conditional, so difficult, so distant?"*

The hits kept coming.

What followed was a relentless series of blows that would test every defense I'd built:

Summer 2021: That summer we found out we were pregnant and then had our first miscarriage.

Fall 2021: Christina's father was diagnosed with kidney cancer. We went to Florida during his recovery.

Winter 2021: My aunt got cancer and passed away. Then Christina's family dog passed away.

Each loss felt like another weight added to an already straining foundation.

January 2022: One of our head coaches quit.

March 2022: Our director of coaching moved away.

April 2022: My third in command disappeared. He randomly sent a text one night that he may need to help with family stuff back home, then said he couldn't coach anymore and never returned.

We found ourselves in a spot where we either went back into full-time coaching or closed the gym. I analyzed the situation, ran the scenarios. I found a gym owner I used to coach and offered to sell her the business. We agreed to the sale on a handshake. We had a six-month plan to transition the business. This was finally my exit.

Six weeks later, she backed out of the deal.

We were trapped in a business I didn't want, stuck in a place I didn't want to live, fixing problems I didn't want to solve.

Like I said, I like to be the underdog. So we revamped the whole team and changed our business model to thrive in this new post-Covid world.

The hits didn't let up though . . .

Summer 2022: We were pregnant again. Then we had our second miscarriage.

This was extremely frustrating for Christina because our "better" doctors told us that after two miscarriages they would start investigating.

Well, once we had two, they told us we needed to wait for three.

The Final Straws

To add fuel to the already raging fire inside of me, another conflict arose between me and my father. This led him to refusing to contact my wife and express his condolences during this difficult time.

This event pushed me "over the edge" and led to our second crucial conversation . . .

> *I explained to him that his behavior—drinking, losing his temper, refusing to contact my wife during this difficult time—was "unbecoming of a man and everything that he taught me about being a man." He tried to fight with me and I kept telling him I don't want to fight. That he's not a victim and I think he's very unhappy and depressed deep down inside. I essentially told him that we haven't had a real relationship since I was 15 and that unless he's going to change and work on building a new one, I would rather not have one at all. We've been "pretending" to have one for years and it's pointless.*

Shortly after this, his health got rapidly worse. By the end of the year he was diagnosed with liver cirrhosis—turns out he was diagnosed years earlier but didn't tell anyone.

Running on Empty

By early 2023, I wasn't just tired. I was depleted at a cellular level. My body was keeping score in ways I couldn't ignore:

- Sweating through multiple shirts daily

- Chronic chest tightness that made deep breathing impossible

- Sleep that never felt restful, even when my Whoop fitness tracker showed eight hours

- A nervous system stuck in perpetual fight-or-flight

Each blow had been manageable on its own. I'd built my fortress to withstand individual attacks. What I hadn't prepared for was the sustained siege—wave after wave of loss, disappointment, and betrayal. Each hit weakened the walls a little more. Each crisis demanded more energy to maintain the facade.

The Protector worked overtime, maintaining cold analysis and rigid boundaries. The Brain ran endless scenarios, trying to solve unsolvable problems. The wounded parts of me got pushed deeper underground, their voices growing quieter beneath the noise of constant crisis management.

I was still achieving. Still performing. Still maintaining the image of someone who had it all together.

But inside the fortress, something was beginning to crack. The very foundations I'd spent decades building were starting to shift under the relentless pressure of life refusing to be controlled.

And I had no idea that all my searching, all my trying, all my sophisticated attempts at healing were actually keeping me from the very thing I was seeking. I was searching everywhere except the one place I'd been afraid to look: **inside myself.**

I didn't know it yet, but the gauntlet was preparing me for something I never saw coming. Something that would finally break through all my defenses and force me to face the parts of myself I'd been running from for thirty years.

The collapse was coming. And when it finally hit, there would be nowhere left to hide.

Key Insight: The gauntlet wasn't just a series of unfortunate events— it was life systematically dismantling every defense I'd built. Each loss, each betrayal, each failure of control was preparing me for the ultimate surrender that healing would require.

Reflection Questions:

- What sustained pressure in your life is wearing down your defenses?

- How is your body keeping score of battles you claim aren't affecting you?

- What would happen if you stopped trying to control the uncontrollable?

CHAPTER 9
The Collapse

You can only outrun yourself for so long.

March 29th, 2023. After two years of relentless hits—Covid, miscarriages, business struggles, family health crises—I was running on empty. The fortress I'd built was showing cracks.

Then came the hospital room that would be the final blow to break me wide open . . .

I walked into the hospital room and I could feel everything shatter. I could feel my shoulders tense and the armor emerge as I crossed the threshold. The lights seemed to dim. The walls closed in. Ugh, the smell.

There was suddenly a pain in my stomach. A sharp twinge in my gut. The room got dark. I felt cold. My hands started sweating with that familiar, clammy sweat I knew so well. I was gone. Frozen in panic. As I stared at the scene I never thought I'd see—**my enemy defeated.**

It was at this moment that I had the stark realization that lying there in the hospital bed wasn't my enemy—it was my dad. His liver was failing. Causing his stomach cavity to fill with fluid and put immense pressure on his organs.

The pain I felt? It wasn't just mine. It was his. Like opening the doors to a floodgate, the pain and overwhelming amounts of emotion washed over me. And as quickly as it came on, it was gone.

When you're frozen in panic you don't feel anything. You're in fight-or-flight mode. There's no time for feelings or annoying sensations. All you can think about is escaping the threat. So as intensely as that pain came on, it left. I was numb.

It was as if someone had severed the connection between my mind and body. I could see myself moving through the motions. I was helping my dad get comfortable, talking to the nurses, managing the situation—but I felt nothing. No emotion, no physical sensation, no connection to the person performing these actions.

The benefit of this is it allows you to handle situations without the emotional distress. So while my mother struggled to comprehend what she was witnessing I was able to play nurse and help get my dad comfortable.

It wasn't until I got home from the hospital that the door opened back up. I sat down on my shower floor. And for the first time in over a decade, I cried.

Ok, I'll be honest. I sobbed.

As the tears ran down my face I could hear a voice I hadn't heard in a long time.

My voice. A different voice, though. My internal dialogue. An innocent, soft, caring whisper.

Then, I heard another.

A sharp, aggressive, stern demand—"*Quit being a pussy! This is what you wanted.*"

The thoughts continued to loop on repeat.

Each loop brought with it a new, deeper sadness. Sadness about things that happened from years prior. Thoughts and feelings that didn't make sense. At least not for that moment.

What was happening to me? I had no idea.

In the days that followed, something fundamental shifted inside me. It wasn't just emotional—it was physical. I could feel it in my body. The constant tension in my shoulders. The tightness in my chest. The racing thoughts that never seemed to stop.

I was experiencing things I couldn't explain. Moments where I'd completely lose track of time. Where I'd find myself doing things I didn't remember starting. Where I'd say things that didn't sound like me—or at least, not all of me.

It was terrifying. Confusing. Overwhelming.

I didn't have the language for what was happening. I just knew that something was very, very wrong. That the carefully constructed life I'd built was falling apart. That the walls I'd erected to keep pain out were crumbling.

The Free Fall Begins

The hospital visit on March 29th shattered the numbness I'd maintained since my dad's diagnosis. I was in complete free-fall. Praying for someone to catch me as I fell.

Somewhere inside me—in that part that always seemed to be three steps ahead of my conscious mind—I was already searching for a soft landing.

On April 4th, I bought Brent Charleton's Correction Method Course—a therapist I'd heard about who worked with trauma. On April 5th, my mom went into the hospital, and by the end of the week, I had completely lost control of the safe place I had built in my mind. The free-fall sped up.

On April 16th, I saw my friend Vince Delmonte's post about the work he'd been doing with a therapist named Annie. The next day, I booked a flight to Houston . . .

At the time, I told myself I was going to Vince's event to network, to build a relationship with him for future business opportunities. That's what made sense on the surface. That's what fit with the identity I'd created—always hustling, always making strategic connections, always looking for the next level.

But looking back now, I can see that something much deeper was happening.

After hearing Annie's presentation, I didn't return to the rest of the event. I went to my hotel to write instead. And there, in the quiet of that room, a realization hit me: I hadn't gone to Vince's event to hang out with him at all. I had gone there in hopes of finding someone to catch me before it was too late.

The truth was, I'd been climbing this ladder for years—this ladder I'd built in my mind of who I needed to become. With each piece of me that broke off, I built a new future piece of me. A better me. A stronger me.

But I'd always known, somewhere deep down, that eventually there would be no more pieces left. The higher I climbed, the fewer pieces would be left. Until one day—no more pieces to break, no more pieces to build. I knew the day would come when I would fall off that ladder. And I guess I was just hoping someone would be there to catch me.

There were only three people my mind would accept as capable of catching me. After hearing Annie's presentation, my subconscious decided it was her.

This is what I mean when I say nothing happens by accident in my life. It's all part of a pre-planned strategy orchestrated by parts of me I'm not always conscious of. Sometimes I'm not aware of the real plan until afterward.

During Annie's session, she spoke about trauma, about the ways our minds protect us from pain. About how we develop different mental strategies to handle different threats and challenges.

What she said resonated with me deeply.

It was like she was describing the exact architecture of my mind—the system I'd built but never fully understood. She had a map to a territory I'd been navigating blindly my whole life.

The Weight of Fifteen Years

As I sat in that hotel room in Houston, processing what I'd just heard from Annie, I couldn't help but think about everything that had led me to this moment.

For fifteen years, I'd been searching for the answer. From 2008 to 2023, my journal had become my most trusted advisor. Through stream-of-consciousness writing, my unconscious mind would reveal truths I couldn't consciously see. It guided me to the right books at the right times, the right mentors, the right next steps.

But listening and healing are two different things. I'd become an expert on healing without actually healing—polishing the armor instead of taking it off.

The real journey began in college with a single book—*As a Man Thinketh* by James Allen. I can't even remember why I bought it, but it sparked something inside me. The idea that thoughts become things, that we create our reality through our mental patterns—it was the first glimpse that change might be possible.

That spark led to an obsession. I devoured everything I could find on personal development, psychology, spirituality, consciousness. I was searching for the key that would unlock whatever was wrong with me, the magic formula that would make the internal war stop.

Arnold Schwarzenegger had been my hero since childhood—not just for his physique, but for his mindset. Here was a man who refused to let his differences hold him back. He showed me that being different could be a strength, not a weakness. His philosophy of visualization and relentless pursuit became my template.

Todd Durkin introduced me to Wayne Cotton's teachings about actually planning your life instead of just reacting to it. Revolutionary for someone running on survival mode.

From there, I consumed everything I could find: The *Go-Giver* series shifted how I thought about success. Carol Dweck's book, *Mindset*, opened new possibilities in my mind. I devoured Todd Herman, Robin Sharma, Tony Robbins (we even attended UPW in 2022), Byron Katie, Steven Covey, John Maxwell, Simon Sinek, Mark Manson, Napoleon Hill. You name it, I read it.

Phil Stutz's tools provided temporary relief—like aspirin for a broken bone. Early exposure to Jung's work on the shadow felt important, though I couldn't fully grasp its relevance to my own fragmentation yet.

Each book felt like it contained pieces of the puzzle, but none gave me the complete picture I was desperately seeking.

The Paradox of Partial Relief

Each breakthrough brought temporary relief—a week of clarity here, a month of better sleep there, moments where I'd think, "This is it. I've figured it out." Then the old patterns would reassert themselves, often with renewed intensity.

It was like being given glimpses of a room through a keyhole, but never finding the door.

Music became another form of therapy. Jelly Roll's raw honesty about his own struggles gave me permission to feel my pain. Mike Posner's vulnerability in "I Took a Pill in Ibiza" captured the emptiness behind success. NF's brutal honesty about mental battles—their words articulated feelings I couldn't express myself.

In business, I watched leaders like James Kemp, Vince Gabriele, and Jonathan Goodman show up authentically—not performing perfection, but being real human beings running businesses. Their example gave me glimpses of what integrated leadership could look like.

The Professional Interventions

As the symptoms worsened, I escalated to professional help.

Garrett J White's "Warrior" work in 2016 gave me my first real tools for self-leadership, but the military-style approach to masculinity only strengthened my Protector. Bedros taught me business leadership from 2019-2022, helping me scale externally while I crumbled internally. Tony Blauer's "Know Fear" work helped me understand my protective mechanisms but couldn't quiet them.

The medical route was equally frustrating. Doctors saw isolated symptoms rather than systemic breakdown. Specialists for sweating, cardiologists for chest pain, gastroenterologists for digestive issues, doctors for sleep problems. Each wanted to prescribe solutions for their narrow specialty, missing the bigger picture entirely.

It wasn't until I found Dr. Leah Teekell-Taylor and Dr. Lana Garner that I experienced a different approach—holistic treatment that honored my body's wisdom rather than just masking symptoms with medications.

By 2020, fifteen years of searching had left me more fragmented, not less. Each partial solution had given one part of me temporary relief while inadvertently strengthening the others.

The Sophisticated Prison I'd Built

By the time I walked into that hospital room in March 2023, I'd mastered a particularly empty form of existence.

I would find broken people, broken businesses, broken systems, and fix them. This gave me purpose, gave me value, gave me a reason to exist. But it wasn't authentic connection—it was transaction disguised as intimacy.

This pattern had become so ingrained that I couldn't imagine relating any other way. The thought of simply being with someone—not fixing, not improving, not strategizing—was foreign territory.

I had built what looked like a great life from the outside. Running my gym remotely. Growing into a mastermind for gym owners. Living what seemed like an enviable lifestyle.

I was very much a student of the hustle, grind, alpha male, go-go-go culture. Involved with the Wake Up Warrior, SealFit, Bedros and Operation Blacksite type of circles. I mastered the art of "manu-facturing celebrity," as one of my former mentors taught me. And for a time, it worked.

Until it didn't.

If I'm being honest with myself . . . Inside, I was empty. I existed as a hollow soul playing a character online.

I lost sight of my true purpose, chasing vanity metrics—money, status, external validation. I sacrificed parts of who I was to become who that world told me I needed to be.

The cracks were starting to show. I was burning out, though I wouldn't admit it. I was disconnected from my purpose, my passion, even myself. The Protector and the Brain were running my life, and the Hero masked it all.

The Body's Final Warning

My body was keeping a perfect record of this escalating internal war.

Every day I found myself sitting in a puddle of sweat with cold, clammy hands. The Protector was running the show 24/7 now. Sweaty hands, feet, and underarms with goosebumps at the same time. A fire in my belly like a V8 engine running hot, no appetite, no thirst, no fatigue. Constantly analyzing, assessing, predicting, planning.

The physical toll was undeniable:

- Resting heart rate consistently elevated, as if always preparing for battle

- Chronic muscle tension that massage couldn't touch

- A nervous system stuck in perpetual fight-or-flight mode

- Digestive issues that reflected my inability to "stomach" my own emotions

- Sleep disruption that mirrored the restless war in my mind

My body was in perpetual fight-or-flight mode, but there was no enemy to fight except myself.

I was simultaneously the most self-aware person I knew and the most disconnected from myself I'd ever been. I could analyze my patterns with surgical precision but couldn't stop them. I understood the theory of integration but lived in constant fragmentation.

Each symptom drove me deeper into the search for solutions, but I was treating symptoms instead of listening to what my body was trying to tell me. I was polishing the armor instead of taking it off. I was becoming an expert on healing without actually healing.

The search itself had become another form of the problem—another way to stay in my head, another strategy to avoid the deeper surrender that real healing would require.

The Breaking Point

And now here I was, in a Houston hotel room, finally understanding what Annie had explained.

What she described wasn't just theory to me. It was my reality. The voices in my head. The parts that seemed to take control at different times. The disconnect I felt from myself. The sense that I was divided, fragmented, at war with myself.

I began to see how I'd created an entire internal ecosystem designed to keep me safe, to maintain control, and to help me succeed. Most importantly, to ensure I was never hurt like that again.

I began to understand that what was happening now wasn't a breakdown in the traditional sense. It was an opportunity for a breakthrough. A chance to finally see the whole picture. To meet the darkness that I'd been running from for so long.

I realized I needed the time, money, and freedom to truly fall. To let go of the constant climbing, the constant striving, the constant performing—and to finally face what was waiting for me when all those defenses came down.

Unlike my previous fifteen years of self-directed searching, working with Annie would be different. She didn't give me another strategy to try or another framework to implement. She gave me permission to stop searching outside myself and start listening within. She accepted every single part of me and let them come to the surface.

I wasn't crazy. I wasn't broken beyond repair. I was fragmented. Split. Divided against myself.

And for the first time, I understood that the collapse wasn't something to be feared or avoided—it was the doorway to whatever came next.

This was just the beginning. The fortress I had spent decades building was starting to come down. The first glimpse of a Truth I had been running from for as long as I could remember.

The collapse had begun. And there was no stopping it now.

Key Insight: The collapse wasn't my destruction—it was my unconscious mind's final, desperate attempt to save me. When all the searching outside myself failed, when every strategy proved hollow, the only path left was inward. Sometimes we have to lose everything we think we are to find who we've always been.

Reflection Questions:

- What if your breakdown is actually your breakthrough in disguise?

- How long have you been searching for answers outside yourself that can only be found within?

- What would you need to release to finally stop climbing and allow yourself to fall into wholeness?

Part Four

Finding ME

CHAPTER 10
Meeting the Team

Out of the wreckage came my first glimpses of something I'd never seen before— the parts of ME. As my mind opened up I began to have visions of the Monster, the Child, the Brain and the Hero. I was beginning to see not just what had happened to me, but the different parts I had created in response.

The Prison Cell

The first vision actually came years before my breakdown, during a psilocybin journey in 2017. I didn't understand its significance then. I couldn't place it in any context that made sense. I'll be honest, it terrified me. What I saw would haunt me for years before I finally understood. But looking back now, it was my first glimpse of the fragmentation inside me.

While lying down trying to sleep a vivid scene would unfold in my mind every time I closed my eyes. Each time the lids of my eyes shut this is what I saw . . .

I found myself standing in a dark hallway. Everything was black. I could barely make out a flickering light at the end of a long, narrow corridor. The faint glow bounced off the rough brick walls on either side of me.

Beyond the light? A black void, pulling me in.

Every time I blinked, I found myself closer to it. Each time, the sound of footsteps echoed louder—pacing, back and forth, back and forth— somewhere just ahead of me.

I was maybe ten feet from the flickering light when the screams started.

"HELP! LET ME OUT!"

The words pierced the darkness, clearer with every step I took.

"WHY AM I HERE!? WHAT DID I DO!? WHY WON'T YOU LET ME OUT!?"

Fear twisted my gut. Every instinct told me to turn around, to run from whatever was in that dark place. But I couldn't. I had to know who was screaming.

So I closed my eyes one last time and stepped through the flickering light.

The air felt heavy. The screams—my screams—bounced off the walls, surrounding me. As my eyes adjusted, I saw something I still can't fully explain.

I was looking into my own eyes. But it wasn't the "me" I know. It was a younger version of myself, no older than nine or ten years old—my inner child. He was gripping onto iron bars, locked inside a cell. His face, filled with terror and confusion, stared right into mine, begging to be let out.

Screaming over and over again, "HELP! WHY DID YOU PUT ME HERE?! LET ME OUT!"

His fear consumed me and I awoke in a panic.

I had discovered the prison of my mind. Inside of it, the part of me I had "killed off." The little boy I locked away almost three decades earlier. Remember the boy from the football banquet? This was him.

Those screams haunted me for a long time. But I didn't have the context to understand what I'd seen. Not yet. It would take another six years—and a complete breakdown—before what I saw would start to make sense.

The Wounded Child and the Monster

After my father's hospitalization, and as I began working with Annie and exploring the fragmentation inside me, I started to have more of these powerful visions.

The first came during an ordinary evening, walking my dogs.

I captured it in my journal, August 2, 2023:

> *This came to me while walking our dogs tonight . . . It was like a visualization.*
>
> *Actually. Back up. It started when re-reading my journal entry this afternoon from earlier this morning. If I closed my eyes, in the memory, I could see a shadowy figure with red eyes.*
>
> *When we went for a walk, that visualization evolved and I could see the wounded child. My shadow. Pale skin. Acne. Chubby face. Wearing skin-tight corduroy turtleneck (they were cool then), tan colored. He's sad. He's been hurt. There's a light glow about him though.*
>
> *Then the "monster" arrives . . .*
>
> *A shadowy figure. Tall. Slender. Less muscular version of me. Still ripped. Veins popping. Red eyes. The figure is totally black except for the eyes. He looks war torn. Like a veteran returning from battle. I can see his scars. Like a shield riddled with bullet holes. The background is dark with a green backlight. Like a horror setting. He limps slowly across the scene.*
>
> *He puts his arm around the wounded child and takes him away into the darkness . . .*

I broke down after writing this.

It was as if something fundamental was cracking open inside me. Some Truth I'd been running from for decades was finally catching up. This scene gave me crystal clear clarity on the parts of me in an instant.

The wounded child wasn't just a metaphor. He was me—the child me. The sensitive, creative, curious boy who got hurt at that football banquet. The one who was picked on for having "man boobs." The one who believed that he wasn't enough. The one who learned to hide his true nature to survive. The one who the world told that, in order to be accepted, I couldn't be me.

And the monster? He wasn't a villain. He was a protector. That's why I started calling him that. He is the part of me that governed through anger and strength. The part of me that emerged to keep the wounded child safe. The part that has kept me safe in Germany. The part that pushed me to achieve, to overcome, to never show weakness. The part that had been running so much of my life for so long so that I would never be hurt again.

You'll learn in *Finding YOU* that we all have Protectors.

They're an important part of our team. Historically, many other psychological frameworks—including the modern Internal Family Systems—use a similar label. A significant synchronicity, to be sure. *How did I know?*

The Brain

As I continued to map my internal system, I discovered there was more to it than just the Wounded Child and the Protector.

There was a third key player: The Brain.

The part that built walls, developed strategies, and used his genius abilities to keep me on track to my goals. Robotic, calculating, strategic. The part that could analyze any situation, find patterns, develop solutions. The part that had helped me build businesses, solve problems, create systems.

The Brain wasn't emotional like the Protector or Wounded Child. It was logical, analytical, detached.

June 5, 2023:

> *As painful as it is to read . . . it's beautifully pure, isn't it?*
>
> *This is interesting . . .*
>
> *It's coming too fast but I'll try to put it into words . . .*
>
> **Breakthrough:** *I purposely flunked the test you take in elementary school for the accelerated courses because none of my friends got high enough grades or were in them.*
>
> **I think I was terrified of being alone and being smart meant I was alone**
>
> **Also, I can see "The Brain" now.**

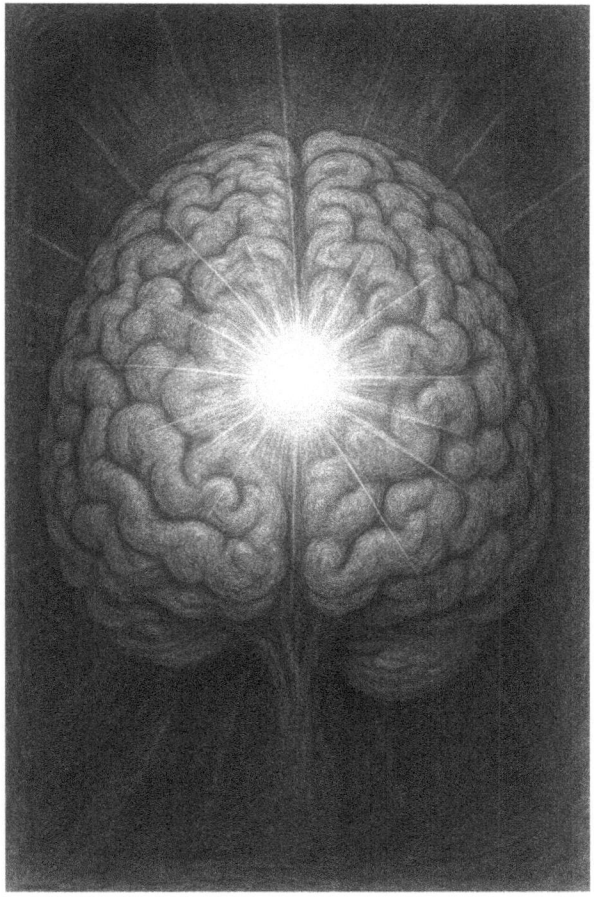

Imagine a giant sized brain that's clear and has the source energy you described inside of it. It's glowing. Hot white like the sun with an orange hue.

I realized the Brain had developed alongside the Protector—working in tandem to keep me safe, to help me achieve, to ensure I never felt that original pain again.

The Brain can see things others can't. Can predict outcomes, manipulate variables, identify opportunities. It was like having a super-computer dedicated to strategic thinking, to pattern recognition, to problem-solving.

This explained my unusual ability to build models in my head, to map out scenarios, to see solutions that others missed. To see patterns and connect dots from seemingly unrelated topics and develop genius-level insights. That ability to walk into a room and instantly feel the energy in it, to predict how people would act, respond, and instinctively how to get what I wanted.

I had this ability to take the overwhelming amount of data that the Wounded Child took in, use the Protector's precision monitoring system to interpret it, make sense of it all, then use the Brain to accurately predict future outcomes and consequences of decisions.

It wasn't magic. It was my fragmented mind at work—each part playing its specialized role in the system I'd built to survive. **It was genius.**

The Brain was both a gift and a curse. It helped me solve problems, build businesses, navigate complex situations. But it also kept me in my head, disconnected from my feelings, analyzing rather than experiencing life.

And it revealed another layer of my early fragmentation—how I had purposely hidden my intelligence, flunking that test in elementary school because I was terrified of being alone. Being smart meant being different. And being different meant being vulnerable.

So the Brain, like the Protector, had developed as both a strength and a defense mechanism. A way to control my environment, to predict threats, to ensure I was never caught off guard, never vulnerable, never hurt like that again.

A Theory Emerges

As I continued to understand the inner workings of my mind, something profound began to happen. I started to see the theory that would later become the foundation of my work. That's how most things come to me—as visual representations in my mind at random moments in time. Often set off by an unusual trigger. Mental images and even full scenes form inside of my mind. The best way I can explain it is as if I can roll my eyes back into my subconscious and look around.

That's how I met "My Team" and ultimately came to the understanding that everyone has their own team. I just had the opportunity to meet mine.

This is how the theory emerged in a shower that would send me on the path to writing this book.

I was coming home from walking our dogs when one of them tried to attack another dog in our building. I could feel my shoulders tense as the armor emerged. The lights turned down. Walls closed in. Time was running out. Before long, I would be "him."

I escaped the scene and made my way into our apartment. I quickly stripped down. Cranked the shower on high. I got inside and sat down as the hot water washed over my eyes. I closed them tight and hung on for dear life. The warmth washing over me melted the armor that had formed. As the lights began to rise, I was surprised by what I saw before my eyes.

An image I'd never seen before. A drawing. There were four quadrants and inside each of the quadrants I could see a part of me.

I immediately got out of the shower and drew the image in my mind. I even recorded it on video because I didn't want to miss this moment.

You can watch the video by scanning the QR code or visiting:

https://www.ryanlighthouse.com/findingme

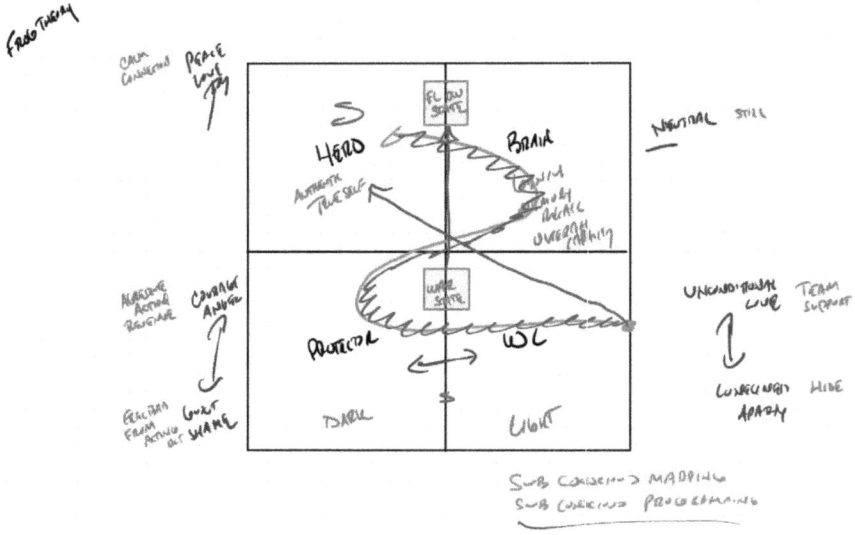

At that moment, I knew. This wasn't just about me. This was bigger. Everyone has their own version of this. Their own team. Their own parts fighting for control.

I didn't have the words for it yet. I didn't know how it connected to Jung, IFS, Walter Russel, quantum physics or any of that. I just knew what I saw. And what I saw was the truth about how we all work inside.

The Superhero

As I continued exploring my internal landscape, I discovered there was more to the system than just the Wounded Child, the Protector, and the Brain. There was a fourth player—one that represented the full integration of all the others. The Hero. The part that emerged when all the fragmented pieces worked in harmony.

I wrote in my journal:

The Super Hero is the best of the wounded child, the protector and the brain. He has the emotional intelligence and compassion of the wounded child combined with the brain's genius for high level of intuition. So much so that he is able to operate on predictable future decision making based on the overwhelming amount of data points that the wounded child takes in. He can use the protector's control and strength to make sense of it all and put it into action quickly. His presence is like a charismatic flow state with an uncommon energy and extreme polar attraction. When fully tapped into this state the hero can intuitively connect and transform into any form.

This was ME. The complete me. The integrated me. The version of myself that appeared when all the parts worked together instead of against each other.

I caught glimpses of the Hero throughout my life—moments of flow state, times when everything clicked, when I operated at a level that seemed beyond my normal capabilities. But those moments were fleeting. Unpredictable. I couldn't access them at will.

Because most of the time, the parts weren't working together. They were at war. Each fighting for control. Each convinced they knew what was best. Each trying to protect me in their own way, but often sabotaging the others in the process.

The Internal War

July 2, 2023:

> I'm stuck again.
>
> It's different than before.
>
> It's like this place of nothingness.
>
> I don't feel anything . . . motivation . . . sex drive . . . anger . . . fear
>
> Not much going on in the feels department.
>
> I tried the harmony meditation this morning and that helped. But, it was only temporary.
>
> I can feel myself transitioning multiple times per day varying from occasion to occasion. This morning, I woke up feeling "ok". Better than yesterday but not "ME".
>
> It's almost like the whole "team" is standing in an open room with 1 entryway. That entryway is a large hole where all of the thoughts, data inputs, subconscious thoughts, overall stimulus etc. pass through.

Each time something passes through, the team fights over who gets to respond to the stimulus.

I can't identify any rhyme or reason why one gets to win over the other. The fight doesn't always happen. I can't identify if there are specific things that trigger it other than stressful situations (this morning didn't make sense).

This was the reality of my fragmented mind. A constant battle for control. A war where the frontlines shifted moment to moment, situation to situation.

Sometimes I could witness all the voices at once, all speaking over each other, each with their own perspective, their own fears, their own agenda:

June 8, 2023:

Last night was a restless night of sleep again . . . It's weird because my Whoop band says that I slept great but I've been awake since 1:58 AM. My eyes may be closed and I may be sleeping. Someone is awake. This is probably why I used to say "I don't sleep, I wait" when I was in my super protector grind mode early on in business.

I had a weird dream too. We had a baby. It was strange because everything up until that moment of the dream had nothing to do with babies. Then all of the sudden someone came to me (kinda looks like my Grandpa) and handed a newborn baby wrapped in a blanket in front of me. I can see the baby crystal clear now. Smaller than normal. A "Premie". The head is larger in size compared to the rest of the body. In that moment of looking at the new born baby that is mine I felt nothing. If anything, I was disappointed it was a girl.

To be honest, I don't care about having a baby. I will. I feel the need to reproduce as a primal drive to maintain legacy and bloodline but I don't have any feelings towards having a baby. If we do, we do. If we don't, we don't. Makes no difference to me.

Everyone says "Oh, that will change", "Oh, it's going to change you", "Oh, it's the greatest moment of your life and you'll never be the same"—I don't know if that's going to be true for me. I love Jax. So, maybe?

Let's just get it all out . . . I think what Christina is doing with the naturopath to get pregnant is . . . how do you say . . . DUMB You're spending thousands per month for someone to tell you to take 40+ pills per day of supplements, do coffee enemas, use infrared saunas, and eat all sorts of weird shit. For what? So you can break out in acne, gain weight, feel like shit all of the time, be constantly tired, miserable, belch constantly, smell differently and overall become less attractive to your mate. Seems smart? After 6 months there is zero progress. Ahh let's do a fasting protocol and starve ourselves for a week for the fuck of it. That should do the trick

Ok . . . Back to me. I am terrified of having a child because deep down at my core I know what my purpose is (although I don't fully consciously understand this yet) and I don't want that to distract me from it. Currently, I see have calculated that the end result of having a baby is one of 3 Disappointment for me in not achieving my goals Disappointment for Christina in me not be the father she wants Disappointment for the child for me not being the father he needs I can't see a world that's different than that. Not saying it's not possible. I just can't see it for me and I'm pretty damn good at seeing shit. Which is the constant knot I tie myself in.

It's so weird because on some days if you asked me I would say I want to run away, disappear, travel the world, have sex with as many different women as possible, live and learn from different cultures, live different places and absorb as much information about the world. I have the money to not work for a long time if I wanted to. I have the ability to block out everything and need no one. I have the ability to chameleon into any place with anyone. That would be undisciplined though . . . The Protector would eventually crush me for doing that. I guess I'll stay here for now . . .

Hey, when you met me in the room at Vince's did you ever think this is what you'd find?

Nahhh, I know you didn't. I know you could feel my pain, but not this. Anyways . . . I'm glad you're here. It's nice to have a friend. Welcome to the show! New episodes air every fucking second.

In this single entry, you can hear all the parts speaking:

The detached numbness about the baby—the fragmented self who can't connect with emotions, who feels nothing when confronted with something that should evoke powerful feelings.

The Protector's harsh judgment about Christina's naturopath protocol—critical, dismissive, protecting me from disappointment by attacking first.

The Brain's clinical analysis of the three possible outcomes of having a child—calculating, predicting, trying to prepare for all contingencies.

The Wounded Child's terror about failing as a father—the deep fear of disappointing others, of not being enough, of failing at the most important relationship of all.

The fight-or-flight mode and constant desire to escape.

And finally, that moment of vulnerability, of connection at the end—addressing Annie directly, acknowledging the pain, expressing gratitude for her presence, for being seen.

This was the war inside me. Not just occasional flare-ups of emotion, but a constant, churning conflict between different aspects of myself, each with their own perspective, their own fears, their own agenda.

And until I learned to listen to all the voices, until I could create space for all the parts to be heard, that war would continue raging, consuming energy, blocking integration, keeping me fragmented and exhausted.

The Map Takes Shape

As I continued journaling, continued therapy with Annie, continued exploring this fragmented internal landscape, something remarkable started to happen. The map became clearer. The system became more defined. I began to see patterns, triggers, transitions that had been invisible to me before.

I created diagrams, drawings, and visual representations of the team inside me. Ways to understand the architecture of my mind that went beyond just words or feelings.

I started seeing how certain situations would trigger certain parts. How specific emotions would accompany specific transitions. How my body itself would respond to the internal shifts with physiological changes—sweating, heart rate, tension, energy.

For years, I struggled with these issues, never knowing their true source. Every day I found myself sitting in a puddle of sweat with cold, clammy hands. When I went to the doctor, they prescribed a medication to block my sweat glands. After that didn't work, I got a procedure done called Mira Dry where they cauterize your sweat glands.

Yeah, it was painful. And $2,000 later . . . I was still sweating.

Most importantly, I started understanding that none of these parts were the enemy. Not even the Protector with his rage, his judgment, his need to control. They had all developed to protect me. To help me survive. To navigate a world that had proven itself dangerous.

They weren't villains. They were guardians. Wounded, misguided at times, but ultimately on my side.

And with that understanding came a profound shift from fighting the parts to trying to understand them. From resisting the transitions to witnessing them. From being controlled by the fragments to beginning a dialogue with them.

I wasn't crazy. I wasn't broken. I wasn't possessed by demons or losing my mind.

I was fragmented. Split. Divided against myself.

And now, at last, I could see it clearly. I could map the territories. I could meet the team.

It was the first step toward healing what had been broken so long ago.

What I was discovering wasn't just psychological theory—it was my soul's blueprint.

Beyond the Prison Walls

The journey didn't end with just mapping the system or identifying the parts. That was only the beginning. The real work was learning to integrate them, to heal the splits, to bring the fragmented pieces back into harmony.

But before I could do that, I had to fully understand what I was working with. I had to meet all the players, hear all their voices, understand all their roles and needs and fears.

I had to see the whole picture, not just pieces of it.

And as painful as that process was—as overwhelming, as disorienting, as frightening as it could be—it was also, in its own way, beautiful.

Because for the first time in decades, I was meeting myself. All of myself. Not just the parts I'd deemed acceptable or useful or safe. Not just the versions that helped me win or achieve or dominate.

All of me. The complete picture. The full spectrum of who I was beneath all the masks, all the armor, all the strategies.

And somewhere in that process, a quiet voice started to emerge. A voice that had been silenced for so long I'd forgotten it existed. A voice that didn't belong to the Protector or the Brain or even the Wounded Child.

My voice. The true me. The authentic self that existed beneath all the fragments, all the splits, all the divisions.

I was beginning to remember who I was before the world taught me to be someone else.

I was starting to find ME.

Key Insight: The different voices in my head weren't signs of problems—they were parts of me that had developed to handle different challenges. The Protector who keeps me safe, the Wounded Child who feels deeply, the Brain who solves problems. Understanding them as a team rather than enemies changed everything.

Reflection Questions:

- Can you recognize different "parts" of yourself that show up in different situations?

- How might these parts be trying to help you, even when their methods seem destructive?

Tool Download Opportunity:
The Wheel of Awareness

https://www.ryanlighthouse.com/findingme

CHAPTER 11

From Poison to Medicine

For years, I thought the war inside me meant I was broken. It turned out I was divided—and each part had a voice that desperately needed to be heard.

The hardest part wasn't discovering the fragmentation. It wasn't mapping the system. It wasn't even meeting the parts that had been running my life from the shadows.

The hardest part was learning to listen to them. To really hear what they were trying to tell me. To understand what they needed, what they feared, what drove them.

For most of my life, I'd been doing the opposite of listening. I'd been silencing these voices. Ignoring them. Fighting them. Trying to control them rather than understand them.

The Protector's anger? Suppress it until it explodes. The Wounded Child's fear? Bury it under achievements. The Brain's constant analysis? Let it run unchecked until I'm paralyzed by overthinking.

I hadn't been listening. I'd been reacting. And that reaction—that constant struggle for control—had kept me trapped in patterns that no longer served me.

Learning Their Languages

What I came to understand was that each part of me spoke in its own distinct language. Learning to distinguish between them was like becoming fluent in multiple dialects of myself.

The Protector's Voice

The Protector spoke through anger, through judgment, through a relentless drive to achieve and dominate and control. His voice was loud, clear, often harsh.

From my journal, August 11, 2023:

> *The building is having trouble renting units. They are renting units on floors above us for $700 less per month. The whole community is pissed. This is unacceptable to the protector. He has countless plans of how to remedy this situation outside the rules of law. He gets obsessed over this stuff. I can't control it sometimes. Then my anger boils . . . and boils.*

This was the Protector in full force—obsessing over perceived injustice, planning revenge, demanding action. His voice was dark, aggressive, sometimes frightening in its intensity.

But beneath the anger was something else: a deep need to protect, to defend, to ensure that no one could take advantage of me again. The Protector wasn't evil. He was a wounded guardian, operating on outdated protocols, but ultimately trying to keep me safe.

The Wounded Child's Voice

The Wounded Child spoke through sadness, through fear, through a deep sense of inadequacy and shame. His voice was quieter, often drowned out by the louder parts, but no less powerful in its impact.

Sometimes his voice would come through in fragments—in lyrics, in poems, in raw emotional outbursts:

From my journal, June 10, 2023:

> *Sometimes I think about you . . . and all of the pain that you put me through . . . and I hate every single memory . . . I hate every*

single memory. Sincerely, Yours with love from hell.

These weren't just random thoughts. They were the Wounded Child speaking directly, expressing feelings too raw for my conscious mind to formulate. He was the poet, the dreamer, the one who felt everything with an intensity the other parts couldn't handle.

The Brain's Voice

The Brain spoke through analysis, through strategy, through endless calculations and predictions. Its voice was cold, detached, often brilliant but lacking emotional texture.

> *I have this weird ability to build models in my head to solve problems and map out scenarios. It only happens on certain occasions. It's like accessing a certain area of my mind that's not always open for me.*

The Brain was always calculating, always trying to solve problems through sheer intellectual force. It could see patterns others missed, devise strategies that led to success, navigate complex situations with precision. But it also kept me stuck in my head, disconnected from my body, from my feelings, from direct experience.

Learning to Facilitate

As I learned to recognize each voice, something shifted. Instead of being controlled by whichever part was loudest, I began to facilitate conversations between them.

From my journal, June 27, 2023:

> *Christina asked me 'Why were you nervous to tell the team?'*

[WOUNDED CHILD] Why is she asking me this? Did I look nervous? Oh no. Did I say something bad? What are they going to think of me?

[PROTECTOR] Why is the worst way to start a question. Did you not listen to me 20 minutes ago when I told you how difficult it is for me to talk about this?

[ME/TRUE SELF] Will you 2 stop? She asked a question. That's what she does. Sometimes they're dumb and untimely. That's also why we love her. Why do you care so much? What does this mean for you? Exactly. It doesn't mean anything.

This was the beginning of integration—not silencing any voice, but creating space for dialogue.

What started as chaos—voices fighting for control, transitions I couldn't predict or understand—began to reveal itself as an elegant system.

A system that wasn't unique to me but universal in its architecture.

Everyone has their Wounded Child—the part that holds our original sensitivity and pain.

Everyone has their Protector—the part that emerged to keep us safe.

Everyone has their Brain—the strategic part that tries to think our way out of feeling.

Everyone has their integrated Self—what emerges when all parts work in harmony.

The names might be different. The specific wounds and defenses are unique. But the structure? Universal.

This wasn't just my map anymore. This was a map anyone could use to find their way home to themselves. The more I practiced these internal dialogues, the clearer the system became.

The Deeper Truth—Who I Really Am

As I continued this inner work, something profound began to emerge.

Each external framework I encountered—each therapist, each spiritual healer—confirmed what I was discovering internally. But they revealed something even more meaningful to me. The strange quirks, weird habits, and what I'd thought were my flaws, were actually my gifts.

The Poison Dart Frog

During an MDMA therapy session, I worked with a Soul Animal specialist who identified my soul animal as a Fantastical Lowlands Poison Dart Frog. Yeah, not what I was expecting either. At first, I thought she was joking. Then she explained:

"You are a Fantastical Lowland Poison Dart Frog. Beautiful, powerful, transformative. The frog lives in two worlds—water and land—just as you live in both emotion and intellect with equal power.

Your toxin is your gift. The very thing that makes you dangerous to others is what makes you medicine. When people feel discomfort around you, that's not your failure—it's your purpose. You are here to transform, not to coddle."

Her words hit me like lightning. She continued:

"Look at the frog's biology. It doesn't apologize for its poison. It doesn't try to be less toxic. It simply is what it is, and that's exactly what keeps it safe and makes it valuable.

You've been taught that your directness, your intensity, your ability to see what needs to change is something to hide. It's not. This is your medicine. This is how you help others transform."

Everything this woman told me about my life through the lens of *my frog* was 100% accurate. She'd never met me before, only looked at my picture. Yet she described my entire life experience in vivid detail. Outlining themes and patterns I had seen but never had words for until I heard hers:

"You attract people who need transformation. They come to you in their toxicity, not because you need to fix them, but because you show them how transformation works. You're the example, not the solution.

Stop sitting in poison just because you can. You endure toxicity better than most—that doesn't mean you should. Your frog was very tired of contending with this discomfort."

The message was clear. *My frog*—ME—needed to rest. Once again, reinforcing the words I'd written to myself in my journal countless times before. Providing the proof to the feelings I've had for so long but never knew how to communicate.

I knew that I was on the right path for me now.

The Voice as Medicine

Later, during a Human Design session, another layer of this truth was revealed.

My chart showed I am an Emotional Manifester—one of only 8% of the population—with a direct heart-to-throat connection. The practitioner explained that I had specific channels opened between my heart and throat that ran both ways.

"Your voice and the frequency of your voice is so powerful to other people because you have a pathway from your emotions to your throat and it goes both ways."

But there was something even more profound. As a manifester, I had something only 8% of the population possesses—**a direct connection to source.**

"The manifester doesn't have to wait," he explained, *"because you have the energy built into you, and you're getting this kind of like direct radio to source, or God, or whatever you want to call it, and that comes into you, and then you can bring that out."*

This meant I was literally designed to receive divine downloads from source and manifest them into reality. I had a direct line to the universe. The messages, the visions, the ideas that seemed to come from nowhere? They were coming through my connection to source.

Suddenly, those strange downloads I'd received as a child made perfect sense. The visions of entire business models appearing fully formed in my mind. The solutions that came from nowhere. The knowing things I had no logical way of knowing. I wasn't crazy or delusional—I was receiving transmissions through my direct connection to source.

This Human Design session was crucial to my understanding of how my mind operated and how, without integration, I lost access to my gifts. I lost access to parts of me.

When I spoke from integration, from wholeness, from truth, that frequency could reach into others' emotions and articulate what they hadn't been able to express. Just like music conveys meaning beyond lyrics, my tone—its softness, depth, timing—could bypass logic and speak directly to the nervous system.

The Recognition

Suddenly, everything made sense. My whole life's picture was becoming clear. The intense emotional shifts that used to convince me something was wrong with me. Now I saw them as the natural result of having such distinct parts.

The key wasn't to stop the shifts but to witness them. To understand what triggered each transition. To learn what each part needed in order to feel safe enough to step back.

The very sensitivity that had caused me so much pain as a child was actually my superpower—the ability to help others transform through discomfort. The parts of me I'd been fighting weren't enemies.

They were parts of a team that needed to come together.

But understanding the voices was only half the equation. As I learned to listen to what my parts were saying, I began to realize something profound: my body had been keeping its own record of these conversations all along.

Every physical symptom, every ache, every moment of tension or release—my body had been documenting my internal state with perfect accuracy.

It was time to learn to read what had been written in my flesh and bones.

The mind had revealed its fractures.

Now the body would show me the path to wholeness.

Key Insight: What I spent decades trying to control and hide—my intensity, my sensitivity, my ability to see and feel what others couldn't—wasn't poison to be contained. It was medicine the world needed. The poison dart frog doesn't apologize for its toxin; it understands that its very nature is both protection and transformation. My fragmentation wasn't a flaw to fix but a sophisticated system trying to help me survive. Once I stopped fighting my parts and started listening to them, they revealed themselves as guides, not enemies.

Reflection Questions:

- What parts of yourself have you been trying to silence or control, and what might they be trying to tell you if you truly listened?

- What if the traits you've been taught to hide or be ashamed of are actually your medicine for others?

- Can you identify the different "voices" or parts within you and their distinct languages?

Tool Download Opportunity:
Meet Your Team

https://www.ryanlighthouse.com/findingme

CHAPTER 12
The Body Keeps the Score

"The body benefits from movement, and the mind benefits from stillness."
—Sakyong Mipham

Learning to listen to the voices inside my head was just the beginning. As I became more attuned to the internal dialogue between my parts, I started to notice something else—something that had been happening all along, but I'd been too disconnected to recognize it.

The conversations weren't just happening in my mind. They were happening in my body. For thirty years, my body had been screaming. I just didn't know how to listen.

I had always thought I had separate problems. Medical problems. Physical ailments that required physical solutions. Excessive sweating that needed procedures. Chest pain that needed tests. Focus issues that needed pills. Digestive problems that needed more pills. Constant anxiety that demanded even more pills.

The sweating had escalated from occasional nervousness to daily puddles of anxiety. I'd go through multiple shirts before noon, my hands too clammy to shake hands with clients confidently. When doctors prescribed medication to block my sweat glands and that failed, I spent $2,000 on a procedure called Mira Dry to cauterize the glands. The pain was excruciating. And afterward? I was still sweating.

My chest felt like it was being crushed by an invisible vise. Shallow breathing became my norm—I couldn't take a full breath without conscious effort. Sleep turned into an all night work and worry session in my mind. My Whoop band would show seven hours of "sleep," but I'd wake up feeling like I'd been running marathons in my dreams.

The digestive issues that started in college became chronic. Twenty years misdiagnosed with IBS, prescribed Omeprazole for "stomach problems," offered antidepressants and anti-anxiety medications when doctors couldn't find root causes.

For years, I searched for answers in all of the wrong places. What I didn't understand was that my body was speaking a language I'd never learned to interpret. Every ache, every pain, every seemingly random symptom was actually a precise communication from the parts of myself I'd locked away.

As Dr. Bessel van der Kolk reveals in his groundbreaking book *The Body Keeps the Score*, trauma lives in our bodies, not just our minds. And as Gabor Maté says, "Trauma is not what happens to you, but what happens inside you as a result of what happens to you."

My body had been keeping a perfect record of my internal war for decades.

The Pattern Recognition

The breakthrough came as I was reviewing my journal entries.

As I read through the conversations between my parts, I started to notice something remarkable: every internal dialogue was accompanied by a physical description.

Every time I wrote about the Protector taking control, I mentioned sweating. Every time the Wounded Child was triggered, I described tightness in my chest. Every time the Brain was in overdrive, I complained about tension in my shoulders.

Looking back through my journal entries, I could finally see the pattern. My body had been keeping a perfect record of my psychological state.

Better than any therapist's notes and more accurate than any mood-tracking app. Every symptom was data, every sensation was communication, every ache was an attempt by my system to tell me something important.

The Protector's Physical Signature

Once I recognized the pattern, I could map each part to its specific physical manifestation. The Protector's signature was unmistakable:

Sweaty palms, feet, and underarms—sometimes so severe I'd soak through multiple shirts in a day. Cold, clammy hands that made it embarrassing to shake hands with clients or prospects. A fire in my belly like a V8 engine running hot. No appetite, no thirst, no fatigue. Elevated heart rate even when sitting still. Goosebumps despite feeling hot.

This wasn't a medical condition. This was hypervigilance in its purest form.

The Protector was constantly scanning for threats, keeping my nervous system in a state of perpetual readiness for battle. He couldn't distinguish between a potential business setback and a saber-toothed tiger—to him, everything was a life-or-death situation requiring maximum alertness.

From my journal, August 11, 2023:

> Last night, when walking the dogs we came across a large snake. Thankfully it was dead. But, in that initial knee jerk reaction of 'oh shit, there's a snake' I could feel the protector take over. It was as if a cloak was being pulled over me except from the ground up. Think potato sack races lol. Felt more like an aura of energy rose from the ground and enveloped my body. As soon the aura rose and reached my head I could feel my focus narrow and all static sound drowned out except for the voices around me. I could hear

every conversation in detail and every sound was amplified. Once the threat was gone it lifted.

This physical takeover wasn't occasional—it was my default state.

The Protector had been running my nervous system for so long that constant activation felt normal. I'd forgotten what it felt like to exist without that underlying tension, that readiness to fight or flee.

The Wounded Child's Silent Suffering

The Wounded Child expressed himself differently. Where the Protector was loud and obvious, the Child was subtle, internal, easy to dismiss.

Tightness in my chest that felt like a band constricting my breathing. Shallow, anxious breathing that never quite filled my lungs. Shoulders permanently raised in a defensive posture, as if bracing for the next blow. A heavy feeling in my solar plexus, like carrying a stone in my core.

The Child was always holding his breath, always making himself smaller, always trying to take up less space so as not to attract negative attention. He communicated through constriction, through making the body smaller and quieter and less present.

From my journal, during a particularly difficult period:

I can feel myself transitioning multiple times per day varying from occasion to occasion. This morning, I woke up feeling 'ok'. Better than yesterday but not 'ME'. It's almost like the whole 'team' is standing in an open room with 1 entryway. That entryway is a large hole where all of the thoughts, data inputs, subconscious thoughts, overall stimulus etc. pass through. Each time something passes through, the team fights over who gets to respond to the stimulus.

The physical sensation of this internal war was exhausting.

My body was constantly switching between different states—hyper-vigilant and constricted, activated and shut down, armored and vulnerable. No wonder I was always tired. No wonder nothing felt stable or consistent.

The Brain's Chronic Tension

The Brain's signature was different again. Where the Protector created heat and activation, and the Child created constriction and withdrawal, the Brain created tension and rigidity.

Chronic tension in my neck and shoulders from the constant mental strain of analysis and calculation. Headaches from overthinking. Jaw clenching from trying to control outcomes through sheer mental force. A feeling of being stuck in my head, disconnected from my body entirely.

The Brain treated the body like a machine that should operate according to logic and will. It didn't understand why the body needed rest, why it responded to emotions, why it couldn't just do what it was told. This created a fundamental disconnect—a war between what my mind thought should happen and what my body actually needed.

I would push through fatigue, ignore hunger, override sleep signals, all in service of whatever strategic goal the Brain had determined was most important. The body's needs were seen as inconvenience at best, weakness at worst.

The Fatty Liver Discovery

In 2024, a routine blood panel and subsequent ultrasound revealed that I had developed fatty liver disease. At this point, it made sense. Just another piece of the puzzle clicking into place. Decades of unconscious anger, resentment, and rage piled on top of an ocean of sadness. Chronic stress, prolonged fight-or-flight activation and the mental torture I'd been living in for decades, can absolutely contribute to fatty liver disease.

My body had been working overtime for thirty years, constantly flooded with stress hormones, constantly prepared for threats that existed primarily in my mind. The liver had finally reached its limit.

This wasn't just a medical diagnosis.

My body was sending me a message that couldn't be ignored: **the way I'd been living was literally toxic.**

My body had never been the problem. It had been the solution all along, patiently waiting for me to remember how to listen.

Key Insight: Learning to read my body's signals became like discovering a new language—one I should have known all along. My body wasn't betraying me with symptoms; it was trying to guide me back to balance. It became my most trusted advisor when I finally learned to listen.

Reflection Questions:

- What is your body trying to tell you through your recurring physical symptoms or tensions?

- How might treating your body as a wise advisor change your relationship with physical discomfort?

CHAPTER 13

The Integration Begins

Leadership isn't just about leading others. It's about leading yourself. You can't lead others until you've learned to lead yourself—**to become Self-Led.**

After months of mapping my internal system, of meeting the parts, of learning to listen to their voices, I faced a pivotal question: *What now? How do I move from understanding to transformation? From awareness and clarity to action and integration?*

The answer, I discovered, was leadership.

Not the kind of leadership I'd practiced in business—driving, pushing, demanding excellence, achieving results. But a different kind of leadership. A more subtle, more compassionate, more integrated approach.

I needed to learn to lead myself—all of myself. Not just the parts I liked or valued or found useful. But all the fragments, all the voices, all the aspects of who I was.

And I couldn't do that by force. I couldn't do it through sheer will. I couldn't do it by trying to silence or suppress or control the parts I found difficult or uncomfortable or frightening.

I had to learn to lead through presence. Through understanding. Through integration rather than fragmentation.

The Framework Becomes the Path

Understanding that everyone has their own team changed everything.

Fear is said to stand for False Evidence Appearing Real, and with understanding it disappears. Without that fear I was able to take my research deeper. It wasn't just a theory anymore. It became a practical roadmap for integration.

I started approaching my internal system differently. Instead of random attempts to "fix" myself, I now had a framework to follow.

From my journal:

> *Now that I can see the team clearly, I know what each one needs. The Wounded Child needs safety and validation. The Protector needs to know I can handle threats without his constant vigilance. The Brain needs problems to solve that actually matter. And ME? I need to be the conductor, not another instrument fighting for dominance.*

This understanding transformed my approach completely.

I wasn't trying to silence parts anymore. I was learning to lead them. The model gave me specific practices for each part:

For the Wounded Child: I'd sit with him in the warm waters of the shower when he was scared. Actually sit. Close my eyes and visualize holding that younger version of me. Tell him he's safe now. That I've got this.

Sounds strange at first. I know. But it works.

For the Protector: I'd acknowledge his service. Thank him for keeping us alive all these years. Then show him—through action, not words—that I could protect us now without his rage. I simply needed to let him know he didn't need to stand guard 24/7. I've got this now.

For the Brain: I'd give it real problems to solve. Business strategies. Creative solutions. Anything except analyzing why I was broken— because I finally understood I wasn't. Switching his focus from fixing to creating opened up my mind to new abilities and ways of thinking.

From my journal:

> *Each morning now, I check in with the team. Who's present? Who's in control? Who needs attention? It's like being a coach—you can't just focus on your star player. Everyone needs to feel seen, heard, valued for their contribution.*

As understanding replaced fear, something miraculous started happening.

The parts began to work together instead of against each other. And if someone got out of control I would tell them this . . .

My Shadow Conversation

Hi.

I'm listening.

Thank you for sharing this with me.

Thank you for bringing this to my attention.

I will always be here for you.

I will always have your back.

I will never leave you.

Your emotions matter to me.

Your thoughts are important to me.

I will always protect you.

I will always listen to you.

I will always be here for you.

You are safe.

You are enough for me.

I'm sorry.

Please forgive me.

Thank you.

I love you.

Would it be okay if we work together?

Would it be okay if we are a team?

The First Glimpse of ME

A breakthrough journal entry from July 27, 2023:

> *Yesterday was the first day in 20+ years that I got to experience the day 100% PRESENT as ME.*
>
> *It really felt great to be present in each moment. To not be overwhelmed with anxiety about what I need to do, what I'm missing, what's happening here, blah, blah, blah!*
>
> *It was nice to have peace.*

This was my first real experience of integration—a full day where I wasn't fragmented, wasn't at war with myself, wasn't being controlled by one part to the exclusion of all others. I was fully present, fully me, fully at peace.

The most profound shift wasn't mental—it was physical. For the first time in years, I woke up without that familiar tightness in my chest. My shoulders weren't permanently raised toward my ears in a defensive posture I'd held for decades. My hands were dry. The constant fire in my belly had cooled to a gentle warmth instead of a raging inferno.

I hadn't realized how much energy it took to maintain that state of hypervigilance until I finally let it go. When the armor came off, I could breathe again. Actually breathe. Deep, full breaths instead of the shallow, anxious breathing that had become my norm.

As I learned to listen to my body instead of override it, as I created space for all parts of myself to exist without judgment, I began to feel alive in my own skin again.

Colors seemed brighter. Food tasted better. Physical touch became pleasurable instead of overwhelming. I could feel the sun on my face, the ground beneath my feet, the air moving in and out of my lungs.

I was coming back to life—literally, physically, viscerally.

It wasn't permanent. It didn't last. But it gave me a glimpse of what was possible. A taste of what awaited on the other side of the healing process.

The most liberating realization was that perfection had never been the answer. It had been the prison. All those years trying to be the perfect version of what others expected had only distanced me from my authentic self.

True safety couldn't come from perfect performance—it could only come from self-acceptance. With the integration of all my parts came the courage to be imperfectly, authentically me.

For that one day, I wasn't just surviving. I wasn't just achieving. I wasn't just performing.

I was living. Fully, completely, authentically living.

The New Relationship

I was developing a new relationship with myself.

I'd spent my life trying to silence parts of myself. The Protector's rage embarrassed me. The Wounded Child's fear disgusted me. The Brain's endless analysis exhausted me.

But a conductor doesn't silence instruments. They don't make violins sound like drums or brass play like woodwinds. They find harmony in diversity, unity in multiplicity.

Each part had developed to help me survive:

- The Protector's strength had kept me alive

- The Wounded Child's sensitivity was my connection to authentic emotion

- The Brain's brilliance had built my success

None of them were wrong. They'd all developed to help me survive. Now I was learning to help them thrive.

And most importantly, I was learning that what I'd spent my life trying to fix or hide—my intensity, my sensitivity, my ability to see and speak uncomfortable truths—weren't flaws to be corrected. They were medicine the world needed.

I was a poison dart frog. Beautiful, powerful, transformative. And finally, I was ready to stop apologizing for my medicine.

Learning to Lead

The path to integration wasn't about eliminating parts of myself. It was about creating a new relationship with all of them. A relationship based on leadership rather than conflict. On dialogue rather than control.

From my journal, July 15, 2023:

> *Yesterday was a good day. We had our O.B. Strong Games event at the gym where about 60-70 of our members came together to compete. This year was definitely different than last year . . .*
>
> *I did my harmony meditation in the morning and gave myself the intention to be Present and Connect. The big difference was 'I*

didn't try to win'—In the past I would say that 'I try to win at the expense of everyone else'. Yesterday, I just focused on making sure my team had fun and felt like winners.

I also removed myself from any of the event logistics. This made ME . . . FREE.

This was leadership in action instead of trying to control everything. I no longer was focused on winning at all costs, pushing myself or others beyond healthy limits, and controlling every variable for safety. Instead, I was creating space for everyone (including myself) to shine in their own way.

It was a small step, but a significant one. A practical application of the internal work I'd been doing. A demonstration that healing wasn't just something that happened in therapy sessions or journal entries. It was something that could transform how I showed up in the world.

Christina: My Anchor in the Storm

The first integration happened in the safety of my own mind, in the privacy of my own experience. But the real test—and the real cata-lyst—came in my relationship.

Christina hadn't just witnessed my journey; she had been my anchor throughout it, holding space for all my parts even when I couldn't.

Even though she didn't know it, I had always shown her the real ME. Who am I kidding? Of course she knew it.

From that first night in high school when I drunkenly told her I had *"special abilities and knew what other people were thinking,"* something about her presence made pretending impossible. She saw through the performances to something authentic underneath. Something I wasn't even sure existed anymore.

From my journal:

> *My wife, Christina, is the first relationship that I've been very transparent with who I am from the start. It's quite ironic considering I don't really know who that is?*

Looking back, I could see the pattern I'd been trapped in for years.

In past relationships, I'd become whoever I needed to be to win someone over. After about twelve months, the mask would slip. I'd grow bored and angry from repressing the real me, then resent them for "making me" play this persona. Which wasn't their fault at all. Once that would happen it was only a matter of time until the relationship ended.

Christina broke this cycle. She was the first person I didn't have to perform for. The first relationship where I didn't deploy my chameleon abilities. I didn't feel the need to become who she wanted me to be. I was comfortable with being ME.

What strikes me now is how she consistently chose to see my potential rather than my problems. When the Protector was raging, she somehow weathered the storm. When the Wounded Child was triggered, she tried to offer safety without judgment. When the Brain was spiraling in analysis, she'd gently pull me back to my body, to the moment, to what was real.

She never tried to fix me or change me. She simply loved me, all of me, even the parts I couldn't love myself.

The Protector had always seen relationships as potential threats. The Wounded Child had always feared abandonment or rejection. The Brain had always calculated the risks, the costs, the potential pain of true vulnerability.

But Christina had proven, over and over, through years of showing up, that love didn't have to be conditional. That someone could see me fully—the rage, the fear, the fragmentation—and choose to stay.

This realization didn't happen overnight. It was built through thousands of small moments where she chose connection over conflict, curiosity over judgment, love over fear. She had been practicing integration with me long before I knew what integration meant.

Now, for the first time, I was beginning to meet the version of ME that she had seen all along.

The Ripple Effect

As my relationship with myself healed, everything else began to shift.

My relationship with Christina deepened because I could actually feel love instead of just thinking it. My connection to my work became more intuitive and less forced. My ability to read and respond to others improved dramatically because I was no longer disconnected from my own emotional experience.

Most importantly, I began to trust myself in a way I never had before.

Not just my mind, not just my strategies, not just my ability to figure things out—but my whole self, including the wisdom that lived in my body, in my emotions, in the parts of me I'd been taught to suppress.

I've been able to watch this ripple effect spread through each area of my life over the last two years.

The Model in Action

As I became more integrated, the psychological model that appeared in my mind was put into action. Every integration moment followed the pattern I'd discovered. My theory wasn't abstract—it was alive in every interaction.

When I chose my team's experience over winning, that was me leading the Protector instead of being led by him.

When I could stay present with discomfort instead of dissociating, that was me creating safety for the Wounded Child.

When I could see solutions without obsessing over them, that was me directing the Brain's power constructively.

The four quadrants I'd seen in that shower weren't some random vision. It was the foundation for an instruction manual. Each quadrant needed different things. Each part required different leadership. And integration meant learning to provide what each part needed while maintaining my role as conductor of the whole orchestra.

This is where the concept of Subconscious Mapping™ was developed. (This tool will be explored in *Finding YOU*.) The process that I used to map the triggers, activators and behavioral/emotional patterns that each part exhibited. This in-depth understanding of the different parts of me is what allowed me to re-unite them all.

The Journey Continues

The first integration wasn't the end of the journey. It was just the beginning. A glimpse of what was possible. A taste of what awaited beyond the healing process.

I still had moments where I'd slip back into old patterns, where the war would flare up again, where one part would seize control. But now I had a reference point. A north star. An experience of what integration felt like, what wholeness looked like, what it meant to be fully present as ME.

I was learning to lead myself—all of myself—toward a new way of being in the world. A way that honored all the parts without being controlled by any of them. A way that integrated the fragments into a cohesive whole without denying their individual gifts and perspectives.

I was coming home to myself after decades of being a stranger in my own life.

And the real me—the whole me—was far more expansive, far more powerful, far more beautiful than any fragment could have been on its own.

Key Insight: The first time I experienced a full day as my integrated self, I remembered what I'd been searching for all along. Not more success or achievement, but the simple, profound experience of being fully present and alive in my own life. That's what wholeness feels like.

Reflection Questions:

- Can you recall moments when you felt completely authentic and present—what was different about those times?

- How might your business and relationships change if you operated from wholeness instead of survival?

CHAPTER 14

Finding ME

I didn't find myself by fighting harder, grinding more or controlling every variable in my life. I found myself through surrender.

I found myself by surrendering to one simple Truth: I was always here.

The journey to integration wasn't linear. It wasn't a simple progression from fragmentation to wholeness, from division to unity, from conflict to peace. It was more like a spiral—moving forward while circling back, revisiting old patterns from new perspectives, learning the same lessons at deeper levels.

There were setbacks. Moments where I'd slip back into old defenses, old reactions, old fragments. Days where the war would flare up again, where one part would seize control, where the hard-won integration would seem to dissolve.

But those setbacks were different now. I could witness them rather than just being caught in them. I could observe the patterns without being completely controlled by them. I could navigate the process with more awareness, more compassion, more trust in what was unfolding.

And gradually, over time, moments of full integration—of being completely present as ME—became more frequent, more sustainable, more accessible.

By 2025, eighteen months after starting the more intensive therapy and integration work, these moments were no longer rare glimpses but increasingly my normal state of being.

The Psychology of Integration

Looking back, I can see the clear stages of transformation I moved through. It makes sense because they are the four stages of psychological change.

The first is **Awareness** and it hit me like a freight train in May 2023.

Twenty years of suppressed emotion erupted. The carefully constructed walls collapsed. For the first time, I could see the fragmentation. The Protector running my business life, the Wounded Child hidden in the shadows, the Brain analyzing everything to death.

I wasn't one whole person. I was a collection of parts at war.

The Unconscious Healing Patterns

The most mind-blowing discovery?

My unconscious had been trying to heal me for twenty years through habits I thought were just discipline:

Physical Release: Twenty years of 4 AM workouts weren't about building my body—they were about releasing the rage trapped inside. My unconscious knew I needed a safe way to discharge that energy.

Building My Room: Every morning after training, I'd sit with coffee and create mental space. I thought it was productivity. It was actually my mind creating the space needed for integration.

Stream of Consciousness Writing: Since 2010, I'd journal every morning. Not for productivity—for healing. Writing is the direct link to the unconscious mind. Each page revealed another voice, another part, another piece of the puzzle.

Mediums of Expression: Video games as a teenager. Music and movies as an adult. My mind found ways to feel and express emotions I couldn't access directly.

Your mind is already trying to heal you. You just have to recognize the patterns and work with them, not against them. These unconscious patterns were preparing me for the next stage of transformation. While my mind had been creating the conditions for healing, I still needed to consciously engage with the process.

Next, **Clarity** came through the work.

Through therapy, through journaling, through working with spiritual healers and diving into the depths of my mind. Through experimenting with holistic medicine, plant medicine ceremonies and alternative treatments I peeled back the layers.

Each page of writing revealed another voice.

Each teacher I found, further proof was acquired.

Each treatment modality used, another aspect healed.

I started to understand not just that I was fragmented, but why. Each part had a purpose, a positive intent, a reason for existing.

The Protector wasn't my enemy—he was the part that kept me safe when no one else could.

The Wounded Child wasn't weak—he held my capacity for joy, creativity, and connection.

The Brain wasn't just an overthinker—it was trying to make sense of a world that had felt chaotic and unsafe.

The point of **Action** is where most people get stuck.

It's one thing to understand your patterns intellectually. It's another to actually change them. For a long time I was able to see the patterns

I was stuck in and witness the behavior. But, I was unable to effectively change it.

This level of transformation requires more than insight. It requires tools, frameworks, deep understandings and most importantly, the willingness to do the work.

The final stage of **Transformation** wasn't a destination. It was an ongoing process of integration. Integration is a way of living. A way of experiencing the world as whole.

Of learning to hold space for all parts of myself. Of choosing wholeness over fragmentation, moment by moment, day by day. It's intentional. Consciously decided. Unconsciously molded.

Healing Tools & Training That Changed Everything

The more synchronicities that I followed, the more healing I experienced, the more ME I became. At my first visit to my holistic doctor's office in Florida the Nurse Practitioner recommended I attend a *journey experience.*

I didn't know exactly what that meant at the time but I had an idea. At my next visit with the doctors who ultimately helped heal my body, Dr. Lana invited me to attend a plant medicine *journey* with a shaman.

I accepted without hesitation.

In March 2025, I met the Grandmother for the first time. I entered through a doorway that had been preparing to open for years.

The Grandmother and Plant Medicine

On Friday, I met The Grandmother. I traveled to a totally different universe. Well, not a different universe. Just the depths of our own.

The ceremony began with heat. Intense heat. My body felt like it was easily 9,000 degrees Fahrenheit. Drenched in sweat, soaking wet, with heat emanating from my heart like a furnace. The plant medicine wasn't just working on my mind. It was melting away the rigidness in my body, preparing me to receive what was coming.

The Grandmother led me on a journey that I have yet to fully understand. While at the same time, can never forget. I was the violin strings on the instrument she was playing. Plucking centuries of trauma, tension, rigidity, and darkness from my body. Using the energy of the sound wave, she ripped out of me that which I never knew existed.

This wasn't some gentle healing meditation. This was psychic surgery.

I floated through an epic story of war, battles, and pure carnage. The Grandmother used sound waves to guide me through pathways of energy in my body, clearing residual effects and collateral damage from what felt like lifetimes of being a warrior. At one point, I was engulfed in the wars of Mongol China and countless battles unseen.

Every time my ego tried to fight her guidance, it lost. She laughed at its feeble attempts to maintain control. The more I tried to hold onto my familiar reality—that fake construct the ego creates to keep us trapped in pain and suffering—the more she showed me how naive I was being.

"How dare you be so naive," she said.

The lesson was brutal and beautiful: **The only control is surrender.**

Once I finally surrendered completely to her, everything shifted. The battle ended. The resistance dissolved. And then came the bliss—complete, total, overwhelming bliss.

I traveled to the moments before my birth as I floated and swam inside the womb of my own mother. Coming to a new under-

standing of the warmth and safety that I had there. The beautiful light and nurturing environment inside of her.

But she wasn't done with me yet.

Then a celebration ensued. A spiritual celebration of my birth. The welcoming of me to this world, in this current body, to fulfill my journey and use my gifts. A symphony of love, praise and joy filled my heart as I came to the realization that 'I am meant to be here.'

Something I once didn't know. Something I didn't believe at my core. The Grandmother showed me the truth that decades of achievement couldn't touch—I belonged here. I was wanted here. I had a purpose here.

This beautiful, seductive and terrifying dance with the Grand-mother is what cleared the way and opened the door for direct access. Direct access to source. A moment in which I understood completely that I am ALL. I am ONE. We are ALL. We are ONE.

In that space, something extraordinary happened. As soon as a question could be asked, the answer presented itself. The moment a problem appeared, the solution was there. I knew ALL.

And then came the realization that made me giggle like a child:

The realization that words were a laughable way to communicate. Too slow. Too cumbersome. It can all be bypassed with the subconscious mind. By connecting to source. When that con-nection is made, ALL knowledge is instantly available. There isn't even a need for thought. You can simply manifest whatever it is that you please.

This wasn't knowledge I could explain—only experience. The Grandmother had given me a direct download of what's possible when all the blocks are cleared, when the channels are open, when the integration is complete.

As The Grandmother returned my soul to the human body it resides in, ALL became clear. Not consciously . . . In a place that I've never felt before . . . Somewhere in the depths of my core . . . It became perfectly clear . . . Exactly why I am here.

What the Grandmother gave me was proof. Proof that beneath all the armor, all the protection, all the trauma responses, there was something eternal. Something that had always been there. Something that couldn't be broken, only hidden.

She showed me that the integration I'd been working toward wasn't about becoming something new. It was about remembering what I'd always been. The ceremony didn't create my wholeness, it revealed it.

Mental and Emotional Release (MER) and Breakthrough Sessions

The proof kept coming . . .

Four weeks after my experience with The Grandmother I attended a certification for advanced Neurolinguistic Programming, Mental & Emotional Release, and Hypnosis.

The Grandmother showed me what was possible. MER gave me the tools to actually live it.

I'll never forget witnessing my first client go through this process. What took me eight years to figure out through trial and error, she accomplished in eight hours. That's an **8,760x improvement**—like compressing a decade of evolution into a single day of clarity.

The systematic release was profound to witness:

Like clockwork, as soon as the anger was fully released—the tears of sadness began. One by one we released the emotions until they were completely and totally released. Once we finished, sitting before me was a new person. Totally new skin complexion.

Lighter. Visibly younger. With a completely different outlook on the problem. It was gone.

This is what makes MER truly revolutionary—it doesn't just address symptoms. It goes after The Greater Problem:

The core belief that holds all the mental baggage together. The one that is bigger than all the other baggage combined. It's the 'THING' stopping you from getting exactly what you want and deserve in life.

You can remove ALL the negative emotions. Erase limiting beliefs. Change misaligned values. But if The Greater Problem remains, you'll still be stuck.

This was the invisible ceiling I kept hitting, even after years of work. Until I released it in my own breakthrough session.

As soon as this was released I could feel the weight that was lifted. The pressure that was pushing me down, gone. The last remnants of emotional blockage relieved. The channels inside were opening up. Literally and figuratively.

The physical reality of transformation shocked me. After my break-through, I could feel a low-level electrical current running from my heart to my throat. Like licking a battery. During meditation, that current would connect to my solar plexus and root, creating a circuit of energy I'd never experienced.

Dr. Matt's response was reassuring: *"You're opening up, man. It will balance out . . . This is so fucking awesome!"*

The physical changes weren't subtle:

- Skin became clearer, age spots disappeared

- Tension throughout my body was erased

- The knots in my chest dissolved

- My voice changed slightly

- Marks appeared on my chest—two triangles exactly where I always "feel" things

The Four Requisites for Change —
Why This Works When Everything Else Doesn't

Here's why most people stay stuck despite years of effort: they're working with the wrong part of their mind.

Your conscious mind—the part you think of as "you"—represents only 10% of your mental capacity. It's the part that makes decisions, sets goals, reads self-help books, and swears this time will be different.

Your unconscious mind—the other 90%—is the supercomputer actually running your life. It controls your emotions, stores your memories, manages your beliefs, determines your values, and drives your behavior. It's processing two million bits of information per second while your conscious mind handles maybe seven or eight chunks.

Trying to change your life using only your conscious mind is like trying to steer a ship by blowing on the sails while ignoring the rudder. You might create some movement, but the unconscious will always win. Always.

This is why you can know exactly what you need to do and still not do it. Why you can understand your patterns intellectually but keep repeating them. Why insight alone rarely leads to lasting change.

Real transformation requires working at the unconscious level.

The Four Requisites reprogram the 90% that's actually in charge.

1. Release Negative Emotions and Limiting Beliefs, Integrate Parts and Do Any Reframe Work

This is the foundation. You can't build a new house on a rotten foundation.

For me, this meant systematically releasing decades of stored emotion. Not just talking about it. Not just understanding it. Actually releasing it from my body, from my unconscious mind, from the cellular memory where trauma lives.

The MER process took me through each major negative emotion:

- **Anger**—Twenty years of rage at everyone and everything, but mostly at myself

- **Sadness**—The grief I'd never let myself feel

- **Fear**—Of vulnerability, of being seen, of not being enough

- **Hurt**—From betrayals real and imagined

- **Guilt and Shame**—The twin demons that whispered I was fundamentally broken

As each emotion released, I could feel my body changing. Tension I didn't know I was holding dissolved. My chest opened. I could breathe deeper.

But emotions were just the beginning. Then came the limiting beliefs:

- "I have to be perfect to be loved"

- "Vulnerability is weakness"

- "Success requires suffering"

- "I'm not good enough"

- "If I'm not producing, I'm worthless"

- "Something is wrong with me"

One by one, we pulled these weeds from the garden of my mind.

The parts work was perhaps the most profound. That moment in my journal when the Protector looked at me with dejection: *"All these years you've been trying to kill me but I'm the only one who's been here to protect you."*

Fuck. That hit differently.

The reframe happened naturally once I understood each part's positive intent. The Protector became an ally instead of an enemy. The Wounded Child became a source of wisdom instead of weakness. The Brain became a tool instead of a tyrant.

2. Create a Compelling Future

Releasing the mental and emotional baggage is only half the work. You need something to move toward, not just something to move away from.

During my breakthrough session, I created the Lighthouse Leader version of myself. Not some fantasy. Not some unattainable ideal. But the real me, fully integrated, living my purpose.

I made it so real I could feel it:

- Standing in my office, looking out at the water

- My son Julian running in, "Daddy, daddy, look what I made!"

- Christina smiling, that real smile that touches her eyes

- My body strong but relaxed, present but not tense

- Leading from wholeness, not wounds

The S.M.A.R.T. goal process (Specific, Measurable, Achievable, Relevant, Time-bound) made it tangible:

It's May 14th, 2026 and I am walking out on stage to an overwhelming reception from a sold out event celebrating the success of my books Finding ME, Finding YOU *and the transformational event series. I am fully embodied in Self as ME. My finances are in complete abundance with my coaching/writing netting $20,000 per month. My bank account is climbing daily and my investments are growing to surpass milestone after milestone. My business is operated simply and in complete alignment with ME. I am thoroughly enjoying my work where I can create passionately and express myself freely. I am more connected, open and congruent with the people in my life. My work is creating an impact that is intensely felt by those who need it most. My writing and theories are growing to a scale that their reach can create a societal change.*

I am leading The Lighthouse Leader movement with thousands of men worldwide at retreats, workshops and in our brotherhood, and we are celebrating the transformation of 10,000 men who have found themselves and broken free from their own mental prison. I have created a new paradigm for masculine leadership based on integration, not domination.

Next I created the future version of me that became a magnetic pull.

Not something I was forcing.

Something I was being drawn toward.

I am in complete alignment with my purpose and sharing my Gift. I am fully embodied in Self as ME. I am more connected to Myself, My Higher Self and Source . I am leaning Into My Gifts To Guide Me On The Path I'm Walking To The Vision In My Mind. My work is creating an impact that is intensely felt by those who need it most.

I am Mentally Calm and Clear With An Infinite Amount Of Space between The Space That I Can Access with boundless energy. I am using my powerful genius mind to create passionately and express myself effortlessly. I am a fully present father to Julian and my future children. I am in touch with my emotions including the overwhelming love that I have for myself. I am able to confidently process and release any negative emotions, limiting beliefs, or limiting decisions. My mind is 'my room' and I can play whenever I desire. I am confident completely inside and out. I experience joy and fun in all moments. I am connected to my body and the powerful energy that runs through it. I tap into it daily and let it guide me. I love my body inside and out. I am evolving daily to become the healthiest, strongest, most aligned and resilient vessel for ME to flourish in this world.

I am fully embodied and integrated as One.

I am experiencing the warm love of everyone around me constantly.

I am filled with CONFIDENCE, EXCITEMENT, CERTAINTY, and BELIEF IN ME to impact the Lives of Thousands of People In a Positive Way With MY Gifts and The Work I AM Creating.

I am inspired to continue to write and finish my books Finding ME and Finding YOU.

I am living my vision, following my purpose, and creating financial FREEDOM for my family by expressing ME FREELY.

I am integrating all of the learnings easily and effortlessly from the Master Practitioner, Mental & Emotional Release and Hypnosis Training.

I am certain that my unconscious mind has those learnings stored forever and I can access them whenever I need by simply entering the learning state.

I am taking action to finish my books, write passionately and express myself freely.

I am connecting with the right people to continue on my journey and those connections will open the doors to more and more opportunities.

I am effortlessly attracting more and more money into my life purely because of my existence and the gifts I provide.

I am building an unbreakable bond with my children through love and connection.

I am moving closer every day to the vision that I have in my mind and am bringing it into reality effortlessly.

I am abundance.

I am certainty.

I am love.

I am truth.

I am free.

I am calm.

I am clear.

I am here.

3. Take Purposeful Action

You can release all the baggage. You can create the most compelling vision. But if you don't take action, nothing changes.

For me, action looked like:

- Daily morning routine: physical training, meditation, journaling

- Weekly therapy sessions even when I "didn't need them"

- Saying no to opportunities that didn't align with my integration

- Being vulnerable with Christina instead of defaulting to Protector mode

- Playing with Julian instead of hiding in work

- Writing my truth instead of my persona

Once you clear the baggage and align with your future, your unconscious mind knows exactly what to do.

You just have to listen and follow the guide.

Looking back on the last ten years, it's when I stopped following the synchronicities and started trying to force things consciously that I fell off my path. My wife, dogs, close friends, businesses, and even my son are synchronicities.

Life can be a synchronicity, if you let it.

4. Keep Positive Focus on What You Want and Your Emotions Become Suggestions to Your Unconscious

This is the secret sauce most people miss. Where you put your attention determines your reality. Your emotions literally become commands to your unconscious mind.

That day in April 2025 when Christina triggered me at the doctor's office? Old me would have spiraled for days. Integrated me could witness it, process it, use the energy:

> After the appointment I could feel my body change. Starting from my heart and moving outward, I began to harden. So, when I got home I immediately went for a walk to release the pressure valve of my mind. The fire was still blazing so I ran, sprinted then did a bodyweight ladder circuit in the 90 degree heat.

Now—I use that fire for production and freedom. To express, connect, create and break free. The emotion became fuel, not poison.

In the beginning, it's helpful to have outside eyes to maintain positive focus. This example from a client really hits home the need for support. Six months into integration work, my client would say "nothing has changed."

I'd stop our session to remind him:

- Six months ago you took calls from the office, not your vacation home

- You told me you played with your kids after school for the first time ever

- Your wife said you seem like a different person

If you look for problems, you'll find problems.

If you look for progress, you'll find evidence of transformation everywhere.

These Four Requisites aren't just theory. They're the exact process I used to end the war in my mind. To integrate the fragments. To find ME.

The journey from awareness to integration took me twenty years to stumble through. Fifteen years of intensive searching. Countless modalities, teachers, and dark nights of the soul. But, the only way through—is through.

The Theory Becomes Complete

For two years, I've been developing my own theory of transformation through lived experience.

The Lighthouse Leader Method emerged from my journals, from recognizing the patterns of fragmentation, from mapping the parts of myself and learning their languages.

I understood the psychology. I'd identified the stages. I knew that integration was the goal, not elimination. I'd developed my own tools and curriculum. But I was still missing something.

When I discovered MER and the breakthrough process, it was like finding the missing piece of a puzzle I'd been assembling for two decades. My theory provided the framework, the understanding, and the map of the territory.

I understood how I traveled the map over the last decade. These tools provided the vehicle to travel at lightning speed.

Now they're inseparable. The Lighthouse Leader Method isn't just about understanding your fragmentation—it's about having the exact tools to heal it. The curriculum you'll find in *Finding YOU* combines everything:

- The psychology of parts and integration

- The unconscious healing patterns already at work in your life

- The systematic release process of MER

- The Four Requisites as your practical roadmap

- The daily practices that maintain integration

This isn't just my story anymore. It's a replicable process. A proven path. A way home to yourself that doesn't require twenty years of wandering in the dark.

Discovering that you're not broken. That the war inside is just the parts of you screaming for attention. Seeing that the pathway to freedom is the pathway back to you. It's just the beginning.

You already know who you are beneath all the noise. You already have access to everything you need. The journey isn't about finding something outside yourself.

It's about coming home to who you've always been.

Because once you find YOU, once you integrate all the parts, once you remember who you've always been beneath the armor . . .

Once you get to live as that person, your story begins.

Key Insight: The war in your mind isn't between good and bad parts of you. It's between the fragmented parts that developed to protect you and the integrated whole you're meant to be. Integration isn't about winning the war—it's about negotiating peace.

Reflection Questions:

- What healing patterns has your unconscious already created in your life?

- Which of the Four Requisites are you resisting, and why?

- If you fully trusted that your authentic self was waiting underneath all the protection, what would you release first?

The Real Story

The real story began the day I stopped fighting myself and started living as ME.

On March 31, 2025, my son Julian turned one. That day, I finally understood what the real story looks like:

> Today is a good day. Today, My Son, Julian, is 1 Years Old. I love him so much. I didn't know I could love anything or feel love like this. I remember sitting at the counter thinking to myself, 'How beautiful is this moment!?—Why would I want to change this?—Why would I want to be anywhere else?—This is bliss.'

Compare that to June 8, 2023:

> To be honest, I don't care about having a baby . . . I am terrified of having a child because deep down at my core I know what my purpose is and I don't want that to distract me from it . . . .
>
> . . . Currently, I see have calculated that the end result of having a baby is one of 3
>
> - Disappointment for me in not achieving my goals
> - Disappointment for Christina in me not be the father she wants
> - Disappointment for the child for me not being the father he needs
>
> I can't see a world that's different than that. Not saying it's not possible. I just can't see it for me and I'm pretty damn good at seeing shit.

Same person. Completely different capacity for life.

This is what waits on the other side of integration. Not perfection. Not a life without challenges. But the ability to be fully present for the moments that matter. To feel love without armor. To hold your purpose and your family without having to choose.

This isn't just my story. It's a mirror for yours.

If you've made it this far, you already know. You've felt the recognition. Seen yourself in these pages. Heard your own voices in my words. The parts of yourself you've been fighting aren't your enemies. They're waiting to be integrated, not eliminated.

In this book, I've shared my journey. The breakdown. The discovery. The integration. So that you can become aware and get clear on YOU. But those are only the first two requisites of change. You still need action and transformation.

That's why I'm writing *Finding YOU*.

Where *Finding ME* awakens you to what's possible, *Finding YOU* gives you the exact tools to make it real. The complete Lighthouse Leader Method. The MER processes. The breakthrough framework. The daily practices that turn awareness into embodiment.

Because knowing you're fragmented and actually integrating the parts are two very different things.

The pathway to everything you want—health, wealth, love, fulfillment—it's the same path.

It's the path back to YOU.

The man your business needs, your family deserves, and you're meant to be? He's already in there.

It's time to let him lead.

Join the waitlist for *Finding YOU* at FindingYOUbook.com

The journey to find ME was just the beginning. Now it's your turn.

Key Insight: This journey isn't unique to me—it's the human journey back to ourselves. You're not broken or beyond help. The person you were before the world taught you to be someone else is still here. The path back to yourself is always available, and you don't have to walk it alone.

Reflection Questions:

- What would shift in your life if you showed up as your whole, authentic self?

- What legacy do you want to leave? The fragmented version of success or the integrated version of authentic power?

- Who in your life will be positively impacted by the healing, return to wholeness and full integration of you?

ACKNOWLEDGMENTS

This journey wouldn't have been possible without the courage of those who took it before me and shared their own struggles and healing. The Wave of Life can only be traversed with the help of a guide. At each step of the journey the universe delivers them to you in the form of mentors, teachers, and experiences. The experiences I went through, people I encountered, worked with, and the books that I studied are what helped me, Find ME.

To my wife Christina, you are the only one who has truly experienced ALL of ME—the protector, the child, the brain and the hero. You have witnessed the transformation and transmutation of me first-hand. From the peaks to the valleys you have always been there. Even when you didn't understand or know what to do, you were there. It's your presence that kept me grounded in my darkest times. Thank you for the relentless support and always loving — ME.

To my family, thank you for providing me with the necessary experiences that taught me the lessons required to overcome each challenge in the labyrinth on my journey. Each of you had an integral role in my journey. For the good the bad and everything in between you did the best of your ability for your knowledge at that time. The foundational set of values that you instilled in me served as a guidepost to assist me in navigating the turbulent waters of the mind.

To Annie Yatch, thank you for **seeing ME** that day at the mastermind event. You've always known about ME since the moment we met. Thank you for your patience, your love and pushing me to Find ME. Asking me to write my story and directing me as I pieced together the puzzle pieces to find the pattern was the spark I needed to escape the dark and find the light within.

To Steve Krebs, hiring you as a business coach was a huge catalyst for the evolution of ME. Our conversations were the first time in my life that I felt like someone understood me and how my mind operated. Joining The Pack was the first time in my life that I felt like I belonged. Introducing me to the warrior way opened my eyes to a new level of personal development. I can never thank you enough for the impact that those moments had on my life and my journey back to ME.

To Bedros Kiuelian, you provided me with the best advice anyone could ever give and reminded me of the infinite gift of genius that was inside with your words when we first met— "My goal is to teach you how I think, not what to do." You were also the first person to recommend therapy, thank you.

To all of my clients from my O.B. Training days—unknowingly to both of us you were the test subjects to many of my theories that will be published in *Finding YOU*. Experiencing the transformation of hundreds of people provided me with the data required to see the clear pattern of the journey, thank you.

To the David Hawkins Institute and the Carl Jung Foundation, Walter & Lao Russel & The University of Science and Philosophy—your founders' work provided essential frameworks for understanding consciousness and integration.

To Jelly Roll, Mike Posner, Mike., and NF—your music gave voice to feelings I couldn't express and showed me I wasn't alone in the battle. Over time it became a road map to identify my mental states and how to navigate them.

Thank you.

—Ryan

P.S. To everyone reading who has not yet completed The Wave of Life and found their true self, opened the temple of the soul and embodied their spirit—I am your mirror. I hope that you can use my story to see your reflection.

ABOUT THE AUTHOR

Ryan Lighthouse discovered that True Freedom is found within. After achieving success in business and climbing his metaphorical mountain top he thought would *fix him*—he found nothing. After years of grinding through sleepless nights, chronic stress, and chronic physiological symptoms the war in his mind broke down the walls protecting him.

What followed was a two-year journey of radical mental transformation documented in over 200,000 words of raw, unfiltered journal entries. He sold one business, closed the other and moved his family south. Through therapy, ancient wisdom, plant medicine, and his own emerging psychological model, he learned to quiet the competing voices that had controlled him for three decades and found his authentic self—ME.

Today, he lives with his wife Christina and two children experiencing the kind of love and presence he once thought impossible. When he held his son for the first time, he finally understood what it meant to truly feel. A moment that would have been lost on the man he was before.

His mission is simple: to help other men trapped in the mental prison of their mind find their way back to themselves before they lose everything that actually matters. This book is his battle-tested map for anyone ready to end the war in their mind and discover who they really are beneath the armor.

He believes that entrepreneurship forces us to face parts of ourselves most people never have to confront and do it at a rapid rate. This pressure cooker of self-discovery can either destroy you or set you free.

He chose freedom. Now he's showing others the way.

www.ingramcontent.com/pod-product-compliance
Lightning Source LLC
Chambersburg PA
CBHW051622120626
46551CB00014B/1914